Stop Obsessing!

DO ANY OF THESE SYMPTOMS SOUND FAMILIAR?

- You tend to worry . . . and you can't get the worrisome thoughts out of your mind

- You leave the house, but go back again and again to check whether you locked the door . . . turned off the stove . . . left the iron on

- You save years and years of old magazines and newspapers because someday you might need an article

- You repeat certain numbers or words in your head to feel "good" or "safe"

- You need to arrange objects—like the things on a shelf or in a drawer—in a certain way or in a special pattern

- You won't use a public bathroom because you might become contaminated

- You get upset if other people touch your things

- You have violent, bizarre, or frightening thoughts or fear you might hurt someone you love

IF SO, THEN YOU MIGHT BE SUFFERING FROM
AN OBSESSIVE-COMPULSIVE DISORDER.
FIND OUT HOW YOU CAN . . .
STOP OBSESSING!

Stop Obsessing!

HOW TO OVERCOME YOUR OBSESSIONS AND COMPULSIONS

Edna B. Foa, Ph.D.
Reid Wilson, Ph.D.

BANTAM BOOKS
NEW YORK • TORONTO • LONDON • SYDNEY • AUCKLAND

This book is not intended to replace personal medical care and supervision: there is no substitute for the experience and information that a professional familiar with Obsessive Compulsive Disorder can provide. Rather, it is our hope that this book will supplement the help which a professional can provide and prove of assistance to those without access to a professional experienced in this disorder.

To protect the privacy of the individuals involved, the names and identifying characteristics have been changed in the case histories we recount.

STOP OBSESSING!
A Bantam Book / September 1991

Library of Congress Cataloging-in-Publication Data
Foa, Edna B.
Stop obsessing! : how to overcome your obsessions and compulsions
Edna B. Foa, Reid Wilson.
p.   cm.
ISBN 0-553-35350-0
1. Compulsive behavior.   I. Wilson, Reid.   II. Title.
RC533.F6   1991
616.85'227—dc20   90-27748
                                                CIP

Published simultaneously in the United States and Canada

Bantam Books are published by Bantam Books, a division of Bantam Doubleday Dell Publishing Group, Inc. Its trademark, consisting of the words ''Bantam Books'' and the portrayal of a rooster, is Registered in U.S. Patent and Trademark Office and in other countries. Marca Registrada. Bantam Books, 1540 Broadway, New York, New York 10036.

PRINTED IN THE UNITED STATES OF AMERICA

FFG   15 17 19 18 16

*To all the patients who taught us
how to teach the others*

CONTENTS

Foreword

Two very important developments have occurred during the last five years in the field of mental health and mental disorders. First, we have made great strides in understanding the biological basis of many psychological disorders; second, serious and intensive clinical research from a number of our leading centers has demonstrated that certain drugs can be very useful in treating some of these disorders.

In addition, an equally important development that has not received much attention has also occurred: Effective, brief psychological treatments have become available.

Nevertheless, it is very difficult to spread the word about the effectiveness of these treatments. As of yet there are no large multinational corporations that are making these treatments available to health practitioners and their patients, as is the case with drugs. Until that development takes place, there remains only one satisfactory method to get our best treatments to the public: the self-help program presented in book form. Unfortunately for people suffering from a variety of disorders, the majority of self-help books present programs with no proven effectiveness. Rather, these programs simply represent the thoughts, feelings, and sometimes "whims" of an individual health professional. But the small minority of self-help books that do present programs with proven effectiveness can be godsends. *Stop Obsessing!* is one of these books.

This book is important for three reasons. First, the programs described herein have been evaluated at leading clinical centers for over twenty years and have proven to be the treatment of choice for obsessive-compulsive disorder. Second, the authors of this book include one of the leading scientists working in this area, Dr. Edna Foa, who, in her long experience with people suffering from obsessive-compulsive disorder, has produced some of the most important scientific evidence on this treatment and its variations. In addition, Dr. Reid Wilson, a national consultant in the area of anxiety and its disorders, has had wide experience in making these treatments as "user friendly" as possible. Third, there are few disorders that need a book such as this more than the obsessive-compulsive disorder.

Unfortunately, very few mental-health practitioners are skilled in carrying out this program since only recently has it been included in the curriculum of medical schools, doctoral psychology programs, and other programs that train mental-health practitioners. Therefore, when this program is recommended to someone suffering from the disorder, the most likely result is that there is no professional in the area who is familiar with it. This book solves that problem by presenting the program in an easy-to-use format. For milder cases, the individual can simply work through the program by himself or herself. For more severe cases, as the authors recommend, it would be helpful to work with a mental-health practitioner in following the more intensive version of this program. In either case, this book may be the best news ever for the millions of people suffering from obsessive-compulsive disorder in all of its forms.

> —David H. Barlow, Ph.D.,
> Distinguished Professor of Psychology and
> Director of the Center for Stress
> and Anxiety Disorders,
> Department of Psychology,
> University at Albany,
> State University of New York

INTRODUCTION

THE CURSE OF endless worrying has been with us since the beginning of humankind. It is the price we pay for being the only animal with the capacity to look at ourselves and think about how things *should* be. Under normal circumstances this can lead to great achievements, but occasionally the ability to wonder, to want, to plan, to feel, becomes an affliction.

- Do you find yourself worrying about things beyond your control?
- Do you constantly think about something that has happened or might happen to you? Do you have trouble stopping these thoughts no matter how hard you try?
- Do you become upset when things around you are not perfect?
- Do you find yourself repeating tasks again and again without a reason?
- Do you repeatedly seek reassurance for these thoughts or actions from family and friends?

Elise faces another sleepless night. Once again the stock market showed a moderate decline before closing today. Each time this has occurred in the last six months, she has begun to worry about losing all her savings in a market crash. And fueling those fearful thoughts are images of her children being unable to go to college, her husband leaving her, and losing her house and job. Elise will run through these pictures endlessly tonight until her mind exhausts itself into a few brief hours of rest.

❧

Just as he was about to shave, Fred thought he noticed a lump in the side of his neck. He pressed the spot with his fingers and wasn't quite sure of what he felt, but it concerned him. His father had died of cancer at forty-eight, and now Fred was forty-six. Could it be a tumor? For the next two days, several times each hour, he found himself palpating that area. His agitated preoccupation disrupted most of his thinking throughout the day. Each evening he unloaded his burden on his wife while asking her to probe the same spot on his neck. Having been party to similar worries in the past, she attempted to reassure him. However, no reassurance seemed to last. Anxious and exhausted, Fred called his physician for his fifth "emergency" evaluation in six months.

❧

Corene's house is always ready for unexpected guests: The kitchen is spotless, the den and living room are arranged precisely, and the bedrooms are neat. In order to maintain this sense of neatness and order, Corene instructs her two children to spend most of their playtime outdoors. Each time they come inside, ask for a snack, or pick up another toy, she makes sure they wash their hands. Before supper they must bathe and put on clean clothes. Anyone who leaves clothes or other items lying around or fails to return things to their proper place can expect a punishment.

❧

Paul appears to have lost his confidence at work. Whenever he writes a letter, he asks someone else in the office to make certain it has no mistakes. As he completes a bookkeeping task he checks his figures six or seven times. At home he has a similar problem—in a ten-minute ritual he checks that the windows and doors are locked, the stove is off, the iron is unplugged, and that he has his keys and glasses. He checks the stove a second time, then his keys and glasses again. Once out the front door, he jiggles the doorknob four times to be sure it is locked.

The world cannot be completely safe and perfect. And no person can expect to avoid criticism or mistakes. But from time to time, each of us goes through days in which we become excessively preoccupied about failing, about losing the things or people we love, about the pressures of responsibility. Eventually we accept that we are not perfect, that it is OK to make mistakes, and that we cannot expect to control the future.

On the surface, Elise, Fred, Corene, and Paul may simply appear to have found exaggerated ways to handle the small irritations of life. But on the inside each of them is extremely anxious because they are unable to tolerate uncertainty and imperfection. For about five million Americans, this need to ensure certainty, safety, and perfection has turned into a continuous nightmare. Robin is an example of one such person.

Robin leans over the bathroom sink, rinsing the soap from her forearms. Shaking the water off, she turns to leave the room. But she can't. Her hands are still "contaminated." Back she turns, reaching for the Ajax, and once again she sprinkles the powder over her raw and bleeding hands. She has spent more than eight hours today in this futile cleansing routine. Before she lays her exhausted body in bed for the night, several more hours will be devoted to scrubbing, rinsing, and scrubbing again. Tomorrow she will repeat the activity again, as she does every day: ten hours of compulsive hand washing.

Robin is forty-three years old. For twenty-five years she has suffered from this problem. It started gradually, soon after her wedding, and was only a minor nuisance for the first few years. But by degrees she became more and more concerned with germs she thought were floating through the air around her and began cleaning her house excessively—especially the kitchen and bathrooms. Her concern with germs controlled not only her own life but her family's life as well. She repeatedly washed herself and her young son. And she insisted that her husband clean himself by following her very detailed rules such as lathering each finger separately and then carefully rinsing his hands.

In spite of Robin's endless efforts, the task of keeping her home free of germs was of course impossible. Her only solution was to seal off rooms within the house so that she could devote her entire day to thoroughly cleaning one or two rooms.

Within seven years, the family lived only in the kitchen and the first-floor bathroom. No other room in the house was allowed to be used. For three years they ate, slept, and dressed in these two small rooms. Finally, in utter despair, Robin's husband demanded a radical change. So the family decided to start over by selling their house. To rid themselves of contamination, they sold all their furniture, including some beautiful antiques Robin had inherited from her grandmother. Their new beginning included a recently built house and all new furnishings. Now the family could once again move freely throughout the house, and Robin was able to keep up with her cleaning.

But within one year, her concern with contamination caught up with her again. And one room after another had to be closed off until they were living again in the kitchen and a bathroom.

Robin has never sought treatment for her psychological problem. After more than two decades the family continues to live in two rooms, only now in a third house. The three children, ages nineteen, fifteen, and fourteen, are still confined to the kitchen with their parents.

For the past twenty years psychologists and psychiatrists have been researching how to effectively help people stop such needless worries and compulsions, and thousands around the world participated in these studies, with great success.

For the most part people have had to seek the help of a professional specialist to benefit from these new discoveries. This has not been an easy task, since the experts are clustered in only a few major research centers around the world. Our clinic receives numerous calls from all over the United States asking for referrals, but most of these inquiries receive the disappointing response "There are no experts in your area."

The *good* news, however, is that many people who worry and repeat unnecessary behaviors can now help themselves. Recent research has shown that written self-help instructions about overcoming these problems can be just as effective as therapy. This book's goal is to bring help for your worries and compulsions into your home. The programs outlined are based on the results of twenty years of studies. The information will teach you to stop wasting your time on endless, unnecessary worries and activities and to begin to enjoy life in our imperfect world.

In the beginning chapters of this book we will help you understand more about the dynamics of obsessions and compulsions. Understanding these dynamics is important for learning the specific techniques we will suggest in later chapters. The more knowledge you gain about your symptoms, the easier it will be for you to take action to reduce these symptoms.

In Chapter 2 you will learn about the more severe types of OCD. Even though Chapter 2 is divided into seven different symptom patterns, these types are not exclusive. Many sufferers experience more than one kind of ritual. However, to help you plan your self-help program, we will discuss each ritual separately throughout the book.

Then in Chapter 3 you will be able to analyze your OC problem. Through a series of questionnaires we will guide you in this analysis. Your answers will set the stage for planning your own self-help program. They will help you decide whether to seek the guidance of a mental-health professional or to follow the instructions of this book on your own. And they will help you choose whether to focus your efforts only on the initial self-help program (Part II of this book) or on the intensive three-week program as well (Part III).

Part II describes the program that you should follow first. It is designed both for those who have nagging worries and those with more severe symptoms. You will learn how to gain perspective about your worries and obsessions, how to let go of your obsessions, and how to gain control over your compulsions. These goals can be achieved by using the many techniques that we describe within Chapters 4, 5, and 6. These techniques will be illustrated through examples, to facilitate your ability to apply them to your own symptoms.

Some people will be able to overcome their excessive worries and compulsive behaviors by following the instructions of Part II and will not need to carry out the programs described in Part III. If after completing Part II you have not gained sufficient control of your thoughts or actions, then turn to the program outlined in Part III. (Or, if you spend more than two hours a day on your symptoms, you will benefit from completing Part III, after Part II. Part III describes in detail an intensive three-week program that has been very successful with obsessive-compulsive ritualizers. In Chapter 7 we present the professional cognitive-behavioral program of OCD, which is considered the treatment of choice for this disorder. This treatment program has served as our model in devising your three-week intensive self-help program outlined in Chapter 8. It instructs you how to devise a self-help program that will assist you in diminishing your obsessional worries and your urges to ritualize. We encourage everyone who follows the instructions of Part III to do so with the help of a supportive friend, family member, or mental-health professional.

In the last few years, several medications have been found helpful for OCD. They will be discussed in Chapter 9.

The last chapter presents encouraging words from obsessive-compulsive individuals who went through intensive cognitive-behavioral programs and succeeded in conquering their symptoms. These individuals offer their stories with the express hope that you too will find the courage and determination to overcome this devastating but treatable disorder. They did it, and so can you.

You *can* get better. Now's the time to stop thinking that your problems are too large or have been around too many years. Become curious about *how* you can change these old patterns. Find out what you have in common with the many people whose successful stories are in this book. And then make a commitment to practice the skills offered. If you are willing to devote your time, your courage, and your determination, and if you enlist the help of those who support your efforts, then you too can change.

PART I

Understanding Your Problem

1 🍎

DO YOU HAVE
OBSESSIONS OR
COMPULSIONS?

MOST OF US are familiar with how unpleasant worrying can be. Driving down the highway, heading to the beach for vacation, you think, *Did I remember to unplug the iron?* You reassure yourself that you did. Seconds later, though, the question returns, unabated. *Did I really?* Now the consequences rise to the surface of your mind. *If I left it plugged in, it could overheat. It might fall on the floor and catch the rug on fire. Then the house would burn down!* For minutes, no matter how hard you try, you cannot shake your uncertainty.

Worries involve thoughts that produce distress and anxiety. But the specific uncomfortable thoughts involved in worrying change from one day to the next. If your boss passes you in the corridor without smiling at you, you may worry, "Maybe she's angry at me." You might even ruminate about it for several hours that day. But the next day you forget this worry and move on to another one.

Obsessions, on the other hand, are relatively stable worries:

The same thoughts, images, or impulses come again and again and are distressing, frightening, and often shame-producing. The individual's attempts to dismiss them are mostly unsuccessful.

The content of obsessions varies from one individual to another. Some obsessions, like Fred's, are persistent worries about becoming sick. Others, like Paul's, are about neglecting one's responsibilities and thus causing harm: failing to turn off a stove burner and setting the house on fire, or forgetting to lock the house at night and having a burglar assault one's family. More severe forms of obsessions, like Robin's, are about contamination, such as contact with germs through picking up objects or touching someone. Still others involve concern about unwillingly committing violent acts, such as poisoning one's spouse or stabbing one's child.

It is no surprise that most of us will seek ways to get relief from our worrying and obsessing, if only temporarily. We hope to undo the obsessions and prevent the terrible, feared consequences from occurring. Perhaps you are like some people who adopt certain behaviors or thoughts called *compulsions,* or *rituals,* to gain relief. Although such behaviors can be persistent, repetitious, unwanted, and hard to resist, they are the only way you've learned, so far, to control the worry. So each time the worries begin, you feel an urge to perform the ritual. Simply put, obsessions are thoughts or images that *produce* your distress; compulsions are any actions or thoughts that *reduce* this distress. We have illustrated this sequence in the diagram on page 5.

For example, after Paul closes his front door, he begins to doubt whether he actually locked it. An unlocked door means that someone could walk in and steal the family possessions, or could be waiting to harm him or his children when returning home. To ensure his safety, he jiggles the locked doorknob four times before he walks away. Compulsions can be a simple nuisance like Paul's door checking or can be as devastating as

OBSESSIONS
repetitive, negative
thoughts, images
or impulses

DISTRESS
anxiety, fear
disgust, shame

COMPULSIONS
repetitive thoughts
images or actions

RELIEF
distress subsides
temporarily

THE RELATIONSHIP BETWEEN OBSESSIONS AND COMPULSIONS

Robin's hand washing. Other rituals include cleaning, touching, or checking objects, placing them in an exact order, and repeating actions, words, sentences, numbers, or prayers—all meant to reduce distress.

Obsessive-compulsive disorder, or OCD, is considered an anxiety disorder. This family of psychological problems includes people who experience general anxiety, phobias, and fears. In order to be diagnosed as having OCD you must have symptoms that fit the criteria of the American Psychiatric Association's *Diagnostic and Statistical Manual of Mental Disorders*; a mental-health professional can help you make this diagnosis. By this definition your obsessions or compulsions are severe enough to interfere with your daily social and work activities, as they do in Robin's case. For years mental-health experts have estimated that only .5 percent of the general population suffers from OCD. But on the basis of recent studies, this estimate has increased to about 2.5 percent. About five million people in the United States are now thought to suffer from OCD. Far more are thought to experience obsessive-compulsive symptoms but with less severity than those who meet the American Psychiatric Association's criteria for the disorder.

The self-help techniques presented are designed to benefit you not only if you suffer from OCD, but also if you experience milder forms of compulsive rituals or if you are an excessive worrier. However, for simplicity, throughout the book all symptoms will be addressed as though they are severe enough to be diagnosed as OCD.

Can Self-Help Work?

Even though many people suffer from excessive worry, until recently we have not had specific programs to help the worriers of the world—the same is true for those suffering from OCD. Most mental-health textbooks, even as late as the 1970s, described the chances for recovery from obsessive-compulsive disorder as poor. But during the last twenty years, many clinical researchers have been exploring the use of a new treatment, called *cognitive-behavioral therapy*, for a variety of psychological problems. Simply stated, this therapy consists of specific techniques that help people get rid of their unwanted images, thoughts, and beliefs as well as alleviate their compulsions. With the assistance of a mental-health professional, individuals identify their specific distressing thoughts and learn how to replace them with more supportive ones. They work directly on ways to stop becoming frightened by their mental images, and they learn to confront those situations they have avoided in the past.

If you have OCD today, the chances are great that you can recover and lead a normal life again. With all the advances that have been made in cognitive-behavioral therapy, about 75 percent of people with severe OCD eventually return to their usual daily activities. Not all of them experience the total absence of OCD symptoms, but most feel that their lives have significantly improved after treatment and that improvement has been shown to hold over time.

During cognitive-behavioral treatment, therapists guide patients through a structured, step-by-step program of practice. Over the past ten years, therapists have reduced the time they work directly with OCD patients, while still maintaining satisfactory results. Research in England found that OCD sufferers who used written self-help instructions, with minimal professional guidance, were successful in reducing their obsessions and compulsions. We have written this book to extend those efforts made in England, for we believe that many worriers and OCD sufferers can overcome their symptoms without direct assistance from a mental-health professional. If you experience moderate forms of obsessive worrying or compulsive behaviors, we expect that you will be able to improve by working with this book on your own. In order to benefit most from this self-help program, you might want to enlist the help of a supportive friend or family member.

The decision of whether to choose the self-help program or to seek professional treatment should be based on the severity of your symptoms. If your obsessions are intense and frequent and your rituals are extensive, we advise you to seek the assistance of a mental-health professional specially trained to work with OCD. This individual can help you follow the self-help steps outlined in this book. In Chapter 3 a number of questions provided will help you decide whether to seek professional help.

Whether you work on your own or with a professional, you must consistently adhere to the program you select. Obsessions and compulsions are often intense and compelling, and your interventions must be just as powerful. If you practice halfheartedly or try your new skills infrequently, your chances to overcome your symptoms are slim. But if you persist daily with a well-structured program, you are likely to experience improvement within a few weeks.

The most important thing for you to know at this point is that you can get better. Thousands of people have used cognitive-behavioral techniques to rid themselves of these problems. We will describe the ways you can overcome your symptoms and will guide you through the actual self-help process.

We know how painful it can be for you to suffer these symptoms alone. Most people don't know anyone who openly discusses having obsessions or compulsions. Until recently, the stigma associated with being obsessive-compulsive was very strong. We wouldn't be surprised if you have not dared to discuss your problems with anyone, not even relatives or close friends.

You need not suffer silently anymore. Find a supportive friend and tell him or her of your troubles. Then, take the next step beyond recognizing and admitting the nature of your problem: Start taking action to control it. This book will help you do that. It is more than hope that we extend to you here; we have mapped a road that you can take toward recovery. It is a road other sufferers have successfully followed. (Some of them will share their experiences with you in the last chapter.) Find your inner strength and then, step by step, take back control of your life.

What Obsessive-Compulsive Symptoms Do You Have?

On the following pages we define the seven most common types of obsessive-compulsive disorder. Read through these descriptions to see if any of them describe your symptoms. You will note that most types are labeled according to the ritual (such as checking, hoarding, or ordering). As we stated early, it is common for a person to engage in more than one ritual.

WASHERS AND CLEANERS are consumed with obsessions about contamination by certain objects or situations. Examples are bodily secretions, germs, disease, and chemicals. To eliminate any possible contamination they will create one or more rituals such as washing their hands excessively, taking long showers, or cleaning their house for hours. Sometimes the washing or cleaning is performed in order to prevent unwanted consequences, such as death or illness. Many times, however, it is intended to simply restore a sense of comfort. The washing and cleaning occur repetitively and vary in duration from as little as a half hour up to ten hours or more per day. The person will also go to great lengths to avoid contact with contaminants. He or she might close off certain rooms of the house or refuse to touch any household item that drops on the floor.

CHECKERS are people who check excessively in order to prevent a certain "catastrophe" from occurring. Common concerns are checking the stove or electrical appliances to prevent fire, checking window and door locks to prevent burglary, and checking one's work to prevent mistakes and criticism. Usually such people will check an object once, then immediately doubt whether they completed the check properly, and have to check again. Some checkers remain stuck for hours in this frustrating cycle of checking, doubting, and checking again. To gain relief they sometimes require others to take responsibility for such tasks as locking the house when they go out.

REPEATERS are those who engage in repeating actions. Once a fearful thought comes into their mind, they feel compelled to repeat some action to keep that thought from coming true. So, like checkers, they aim to prevent or neutralize possible catastrophes. However, unlike checkers, repeaters cannot identify a logical connection between the obsession and the compulsion. In fact, a magical quality is often present in their thinking, such as the idea of preventing a spouse from dying by dressing and undressing repeatedly until the thought of the possible death stops.

ORDERERS are people who require that things around them be arranged in certain rigid ways, including symmetrical patterns. For instance, they may require that they make the bed impeccably, without a single wrinkle. Or they might lay out their daily vitamins in a special design on the kitchen counter and rearrange that design each time they remove a pill. Orderers spend a great deal of time making sure things are in the "right place" and notice immediately when any pattern has been disrupted. Often they will become extremely upset if anyone else has rearranged their possessions. Usually orderers do not fear impending disaster. Rather, they are compelled to engage in the ritualistic action by a general sense of discomfort that arises when things are not presented "perfectly."

HOARDERS collect trivial objects and find it impossible to rid themselves of these possessions. A hoarder might walk the street and collect small pieces of paper, storing them at home in case he or she needs them sometime in the future. While others consider the collections to be useless, the hoarder deems them of great value. Some individuals will collect newspapers for decades in case they need a specific article. In severe cases, the person's entire house is so filled with such collections that additional space needs to be rented.

THINKING RITUALIZERS usually enlist repetitive thoughts or images, called thinking compulsions, in order to counteract their anxiety-provoking thoughts or images, the obsessions.

On the surface, thinking ritualizers may seem similar to pure obsessionals, since both have repetitive thoughts and no behavioral rituals. But the thoughts of pure obsessionals *create* anxiety and distress, while the thinking ritualizers have obsessions as well as thinking rituals that *reduce* the obsessional distress. The patterns of thinking ritualizers are similar to those of repeaters, but their focus is on repetitious ritualistic *thoughts* instead of *behaviors*. The most common rituals are praying, repeating certain words or phrases, and counting. Stewart, for example, believed that the number three would bring him bad luck and the number six was good luck. Whenever a thought that included the number three entered his mind, Stewart repeated the number six several times to prevent bad luck. Thinking ritualizers will also try to recall events in detail or repeat a mental list as a way to ensure safety. For instance, Dan, a sixty-seven-year-old, spent hours each day testing his memory by trying to remember unimportant events—to convince himself that he was not developing Alzheimer's disease.

WORRIERS AND PURE OBSESSIONALS experience repetitious negative thoughts that are uncontrollable and quite upsetting. However, unlike those with the other types of OCD, they do not engage in repetitious behaviors such as washing hands or checking door locks, nor do they have thinking compulsions such as praying or counting. Their worries can focus on the simplest everyday occurrences or on frightening, violent, even shameful thoughts. Common examples are dwelling on health-related problems or past traumatic events, or worrying about failing at some future task. Elise, who was mentioned in the introduction, spent hours each day worrying about losing all her savings in the market crash and being unable to educate her children. But she did not develop any compulsive behavior that could temporarily alleviate her distress. More severe examples include shameful images of inappropriate sexual behavior, or impulses to kill or hurt themselves or loved ones. For hours or sometimes days afterward the person may dwell on how these thoughts might come true.

The following questionnaire will help you identify the types of problems that most trouble you. Read through the statements listed and check the ones that are true for you. If you check *two* or more items in any group, this is an indication that you should specifically address those concerns in your self-help program. Don't be surprised if you check more than one item in *several* groups. Many people have more than one type of OCD symptoms.

UNDERSTANDING YOUR PROBLEM

A. *What Symptoms Bother You?*
   Place a check by each item that has troubled you in the last month.

Washing and Cleaning

_____ 1. I avoid touching certain things because of possible contamination.
_____ 2. I have difficulty picking up items that have dropped on the floor.
_____ 3. I clean my household excessively.
_____ 4. I wash my hands excessively.
_____ 5. I often take extremely long showers or baths.
_____ 6. I'm overly concerned with germs and diseases.

Checking and Repeating

_____ 1. I frequently have to check things over and over again.
_____ 2. I have difficulty finishing things because I repeat actions.
_____ 3. I often repeat actions in order to prevent something bad from happening.
_____ 4. I worry excessively about making mistakes.

_____ 5. I worry excessively that someone will get harmed because of me.

_____ 6. Certain thoughts that come into my mind make me do things over and over again.

Ordering

_____ 1. I must have certain things around me set in a specific order.

_____ 2. I spend much time making sure that things are in the right place.

_____ 3. I notice immediately when my things are out of place.

_____ 4. It is important that my bed is straightened out impeccably.

_____ 5. I need to arrange certain things in special patterns.

_____ 6. When my things are rearranged by others, I get extremely upset.

Hoarding

_____ 1. I have difficulty throwing things away.

_____ 2. I find myself bringing home seemingly useless materials.

_____ 3. Over the years my home has become cluttered with collections.

_____ 4. I do not like other people to touch my possessions.

_____ 5. I find myself unable to get rid of things.

_____ 6. Other people think my collections are useless.

Thinking Rituals

_____ 1. Repeating certain words or numbers in my head makes me feel good.

_____ 2. I often have to say certain things to myself again and again in order to feel safe.

_____ 3. I find myself spending a lot of time praying for nonreligious purposes.

_____ 4. "Bad" thoughts force me to think about "good" thoughts.

_____ 5. I try to remember events in detail or make mental lists to prevent unpleasant consequences.

_____ 6. The only way I can stay calm at times is by thinking the "right" things.

Worries and Pure Obsessions

While I do not engage in any behavorial or thinking rituals:

_____ 1. I often get upset by unpleasant thoughts that come into my mind against my will.

_____ 2. I usually have doubts about the simple everyday things I do.

_____ 3. I have no control over my thoughts.

_____ 4. Frequently the things that pop into my mind are shameful, frightening, violent, or bizarre.

_____ 5. I'm afraid that my bad thoughts will come true.

_____ 6. When I start to worry I cannot easily stop.

_____ 7. Little, insignificant events make me worry excessively.

B. *In the past month, how much time have you spent, on an average day, engaged in these symptoms?*

	Hours	Minutes
Washing and Cleaning	_____	_____
Checking and Repeating	_____	_____
Ordering	_____	_____
Hoarding	_____	_____
Thinking Rituals	_____	_____
Worrying or Obsessing	_____	_____

Now total up the number of hours and minutes you listed in part B. If you spend more than two hours each day obsessing or ritualizing in any type of symptoms, you may need professional help in guiding you through this program. We will assist you in making that decision in Chapter 3.

Common Features of Obsessive-Compulsives

To prepare you for the self-help program outlined in the book, we first would like to help you understand the disorder. In this section we will describe seven traits common in people who have obsessions and compulsions. The first three are related to obsessions and worrying in general; the last four concern those who experience obsessions and compulsions. Not all characteristics are experienced by every individual, so don't be surprised if you recognize only some. As you identify the tendencies relevant to you, you will begin to better understand your own symptoms.

1. *Your worries and obsessions involve a concern with disastrous consequences.* The persistent distress that accompanies an obsession often reflects a fear of harm that will befall you or others. For instance, the person worried about money might imagine losing his or her job, then not being able to make the monthly payments on debts. The mortgage company will repossess the house, the bank will repossess the car. This will mean living in a small apartment and riding the bus to work. But the bus route isn't convenient to many jobs. As a result, he or she will be unemployed for months and possibly end up in the streets.

A checker will usually have this same kind of fear about the horrible consequences of mistakes or carelessness. When asked what is causing this checking, a characteristic answer is "I am checking the doors and windows because I don't want anyone to break in, kill my children, and take all of my possessions. If that happens, it will be my fault, and people will blame me for being irresponsible." Another checker might say, "If I don't check my typing seven or eight times, my boss will point out all my mistakes, and I'll feel ashamed." Similarly, a washer often focuses on some dreaded effects of contact with dirt or contamination. "What if I didn't wash enough? Will I be sick? Am I going to make other people sick? What if I touched something and didn't wash?"

2. *There are times when you know that your obsessions are irrational.* Most worriers and OC's would agree that their obsessions are senseless. During times when they are not troubled by their symptoms, they acknowledge they probably won't become penniless, be humiliated by their boss if they make a typing error, or get sick by failing to wash their hands five times. Nonetheless, when they begin their worrying, they dread those possibilities.

A few, however, truly believe that their fears are rooted in reality. For example, Anthony was obsessed with the thought that he was going to contract leukemia through exposure to leukemia victims and infect his children and wife with this disease. After his father visited a friend in the hospital, Anthony believed his father was contaminated with leukemia germs. Since he and his father went to the same dentist, he believed his father had passed the germs to the dentist. Consequently, Anthony stopped visiting that dentist. He was 100 percent certain that if he returned to the dentist's office he would infect his own family with fatal leukemia.

3. *You try to resist your obsessions, but that only makes them worse.* Because obsessional thoughts or images provoke so much distress or fear, you want to get rid of them. When a thought is terrifying, naturally you do all you can to suppress it. But by fighting the thought, you end up encouraging its persistence.

This means your obsessions are maintained in part through paradox: The more you fight them, the more difficult it is for you to dismiss them. But the more you actively resist them, the more stubborn they seem to get. A similar dilemma is experienced by insomniacs: The harder they try to fall asleep, the less they are able to fall asleep.

Why is this? When you resist a thought, you establish a

special "relationship" with it, a relationship of opposites. Remember what happens when you place the north end of a bar magnet next to the south end of another one? Opposites attract! When you become afraid to have a specific thought again, your body moves into a defensive mode and produces a chemical called *epinephrine*. Epinephrine prepares you to fight: Your muscles tense, your heart rate increases, breathing increases, and *your thoughts begin to race*. And what thoughts are naturally going to race through your mind? How not to have that obsession again! By becoming scared and trying to prevent those worried thoughts from occurring again, your body's response actually brings those thoughts back to mind.

Here is a partial list of the ways your thoughts and actions can encourage obsessions to return:

- if you fear your obsessions
- if you actively fight against them
- if you struggle to avoid any situation that might remind you of them
- if you set a goal of "never ever" having another obsession
- if you worry about the next time you might have an obsession.

Each of these actions invites your fearful thoughts to return by creating a dynamic tension between you and your obsessions. Becoming aware of this paradoxical nature of your obsessions can be a cornerstone in controlling them. As you learn ways to stop fighting your obsessive thoughts, those thoughts will diminish in frequency and intensity. We will teach you how to do that in Chapter 5.

4. *Compulsive rituals provide you with temporary relief.* If you worry that you are going to accidentally leave your kitchen stove on, the best thing you can do is to check to make sure that it's off before you leave the house. If you are a person

who has horrendous repeated images about how the unattended burner on high heat will somehow result in the house burning down, then you will feel an even greater urgency to ensure that the stove is off. One glance at the burner knob may not do the trick, since your feared consequence is so intensely present in your mind. In these situations, some people develop specific patterns of action in order to reduce their anxiety. For example, they might touch each knob of the stove five times while subvocalizing the numbers. If done correctly, they then feel safe enough to leave the house. But the next time they prepare to leave, they may feel compelled to repeat this identical pattern.

Imagine Chris, the father of a two-year-old child, setting the table for a family dinner. Standing at the dining room table, placing the utensils, he suddenly experiences an impulse to kill his son. This impulse horrifies him. Over time, as it recurs frequently, Chris devises special ways to end the intolerable fright. For example, if he repeats the behavior in which he was engaged at the moment of the obsessive impulse, he can then "erase" the obsession. So if the impulse were to reoccur while Chris was setting the table, he would collect the silverware, walk out of the room, reenter, and carefully set the table again. And he would do it again and again until the impulse disappeared. It would be only then that he could sigh with relief, "It won't come true now, because I've erased it." Each time the obsession returns Chris will use this same action again to "undo" the impulse and relieve his anxiety and guilt.

These two examples illustrate that the fear, shame, and guilt caused by an obsession can be so traumatizing that the person experiencing them will desperately seek relief. The compulsive ritual provides such relief and restores a sense of relative safety, even if just for a little while. The relief provided by the compulsive behaviors motivates use of them again and again. But they never provide a long-lasting solution. Soon the obsessions will spring back, and the whole sequence will have to be repeated.

5. *Your rituals usually involve specific sequences.* To end the distress of obsessions, typically a person must perform the compulsive behaviors in a certain ritualized manner. Checkers who worry about forgetting some safety precaution when leaving their house may create such a set pattern. For instance, Charles checks each window, starting from the northeast corner of the house and ending in the kitchen. There he scans every appliance in a clockwise direction. He presses on the refrigerator and freezer doors, lays the toaster cord on top of the toaster, runs his hand across each empty electrical outlet, and touches each stove and oven knob. He pulls his keys out of his pocket and holds them in his left hand. After he steps out of the front door, he must look again at the keys in his hand before closing and locking the door. Then he inserts the key in the dead bolt and listens for its usual clicking sound as he locks and unlocks the dead bolt three times, just to be sure.

Washers who have more serious problems with OCD may feel compelled to take a shower. But they will not simply take frequent long ones. Their showers will tend to be elaborate and include certain sequences and repetitions to ensure maximum cleanliness. If they feel contaminated by "floor germs," they will wash their head first and work their way systematically down to their legs. This is to prevent the spread of germs from the legs, which are closer to the floor, to other parts of the body. On the other hand, if they fear contamination by feces and urine, they will start by washing their head, arms, and chest, then continue with their feet and legs, leaving their genital and anal areas for last.

Likewise, special routines are developed for hand washing. These include washing each finger separately a specific number of times and scrubbing under the nails and the area between the fingers. To be effective, this ritualistic sequence of actions usually needs to be completed without disturbance. If someone interrupts the sequence, or if the person forgets what step of the sequence has been completed, the entire ritual must be repeated.

Unlike most people, OC's are often not satisfied with washing their hands once or checking the door once to feel safe. They feel compelled to repeat the action over and over. For example, if on her way to the beach a checker starts to doubt whether she unplugged the iron, she will most likely return home to check to make sure she unplugged it. She will enter the room, notice with relief that the plug is already out of the socket, then leave the room. Two steps out of the door, she will doubt her memory and return for a second checking. In severe cases, that pattern might be repeated for hours. Since obsessive thoughts and images tend to enter the OC's mind many times during the day, her life often gets consumed with long, elaborate rituals.

6. *You try to resist the compulsions too.* If a ritual is brief and doesn't interfere with daily living, then many people can simply tolerate it. For instance, we all know people who, before leaving their home, must check their briefcase or purse for reading glasses, keys, makeup, and other objects they think they may need. It is not enough for them to check once; they need to check two or three times. However, checking a briefcase three times doesn't take more than five minutes, so such symptoms are not severely debilitating, even if they are bothersome.

But in severe cases the compulsions are quite debilitating. They can become so distressing that some OC's wish to stop them altogether. Washing one's hands until they bleed is obviously abhorrent, and, thus, some washers will go to great lengths in order to delay washing. Others will avoid touching anything in order to avoid washing. If they are having extreme difficulty, obsessive-compulsives will stop all their daily activities in order to stop ritualizing. One washer, for example, feared contamination by "death germs," and was washing and cleaning endlessly. The rituals became so distressing that she finally chose to never leave her bed.

7. *You seek out others to help with your rituals.* Many times people with severe OCD will enlist the help of others in their search for relief. Some, like Marge, will seek direct verbal reassurance. Marge, a twenty-nine-year-old divorcée, was obsessed with the idea that if her son became sick, she might not take him to the doctor in time and he would die. Driven by this fear, Marge checked his temperature repeatedly and watched his every move in search of early signs of illness. Any slight cough would provoke her to call his pediatrician for reassurance. Such telephone calls would pacify her anxiety temporarily. But within a few hours, Marge would find herself calling the doctor again with a new concern. She also phoned the poison-control center almost daily, worried about her son touching the laundry detergent, the dishwasher detergent, or dishes that might not have been rinsed enough.

Marge did not trust her ability to make the right decision regarding her son's safety and sought guidance from others. Such seeking of reassurance is a type of ritual, and like all rituals is designed to reduce obsessional worry.

Another way in which OC's involve others in their symptom pattern is by requesting that they assist the sufferer in performing rituals or that they perform rituals in place of the sufferer. For instance, washers often ask that their spouse and children wash and clean excessively. Checkers might assign family members the responsibility of checking the doors and windows. Once having delegated the responsibility, they feel relatively free of that obsession.

Tony, a fifteen-year-old boy, felt compelled to check many items in his home, including locked doors, windows, specific placement of items in the refrigerator, the location of books, and any objects on flat surfaces. Because this routine caused him enormous distress if done alone, Tony requested that his mother perform these rituals with him. In this way, he could be certain that he accomplished each and every task.

Some washers will ask family members to count how many times they have washed their hands. If a person feels compelled to wash exactly forty times in a row, and if losing count means that he must start over again, then accuracy becomes essential. Therefore, family members are appointed to count and to reassure that the task has been completed correctly.

What Causes Obsessive-Compulsive Symptoms?

Certainly you have asked yourself, "How did I become a professional worrier?" The answer is not simple. While much is now known about the treatment of worries and obsessions, researchers and mental-health professionals still do not know much about their causes.

Several theories suggest a biological basis for the disorder, and a number of studies are currently exploring this possibility. Positron emission transaxial tomography (PETT) and other brain-imaging techniques have suggested that there may be some abnormalities in the frontal lobe and the basal ganglia that influence OCD symptoms. Other studies seem to indicate that abnormalities in certain neurotransmitters, the brain's messengers, may be involved. One is serotonin, a neurotransmitter that is thought to help regulate mood, aggression, and impulsivity. Neurons that respond to serotonin are found throughout the brain but especially in the frontal lobes and the basal ganglia. Medications that influence the uptake of serotonin seem especially helpful in the treatment of OCD.

Don't be concerned by the idea that OCD symptoms might have a biological basis. Researchers know that psychological treatment can alter patterns that stem, in part, from a biological base. Numerous studies, for instance, have shown that through conditioning we can train animals to act against their built-in instincts. And, secondly, our thoughts, emotions, and behaviors may *influence* our brain chemistry over time, so that the abnormalities that sometimes appear on brain-imaging scans of OCD sufferers may be the result of long-term obsessions and compulsions rather than their cause.

Does OCD run in families? The studies that have researched family history offer no definite clues. They have found that relatives of OC's are more likely than the average person to have anxiety or depression problems. But, surprisingly, only a small number of parents of OC's also suffer from the same disorder. It is hard to estimate the occurrence of OCD in family history, since sufferers have tended to keep their disorder a secret, even from their loved ones.

Studies of life histories of obsessive-compulsives are not more revealing. No particular childhood events distinguish OCD sufferers from others. In fact, almost all children develop certain briefly held rituals to "protect" themselves and their loved ones. They avoid "stepping on a crack and breaking Mommy's back." Or they repeat the same prayer again and again to make sure Mom and Dad don't get hurt. They hold their breath over bridges, lift their feet over railroad tracks, and are quiet as they pass the cemetery so as not to wake the dead. As with phobias, for most children these magical protective rituals fade away in time. Only a few children develop symptoms pervasive enough to be diagnosed as OCD.

It is in the late teenage years and the early twenties that OCD usually begins to surface. Why is this age group more vulnerable to the development of these symptoms? Obsessive-compulsives tend to worry about hurting themselves or others by neglecting their responsibilities, and it's in the late teens and early twenties that personal responsibility increases. One looks for employment and considers getting married, having children, and financially supporting a family. With increased responsibilities there are more opportunities to make mistakes that can lead to serious consequences. People who develop OCD tend to exaggerate the likelihood of such mistakes as well as their importance. When most people would perceive the negative outcome of a particular decision as troublesome, the OC would view it as devastating. Perhaps the increased responsibility during young adulthood gives rise to OC symptoms in those who are predisposed to the disorder.

Once OCD symptoms begin, they usually become increasingly more pervasive over time. Some people don't remember the more subtle onset of the symptoms, and report that they became severely disturbed within several days or weeks. Many sufferers, however, describe some event or thought that they associate with a substantial increase in their obsessions and compulsions. For example, one person remembered hearing a story on AIDS, and soon after he began to dwell on contracting the AIDS virus himself. To protect himself from this terrible fate, he rapidly increased his daily hand washing and started to avoid people who might carry the AIDS virus.

It is hard to understand why one would continue to think or imagine things that are so painful. Experts in OCD have proposed several psychological explanations. One is that by keeping one's mind focused on certain obsessions, a person can unconsciously avoid more unpleasant thoughts. For example, Joel, whom we will discuss in Chapter 2, was preoccupied with worries about his impulses to kill his daughter. These worries may have covered up his ambivalent feelings about being a father. Acknowledging such feelings may have caused Joel more distress than the impulse to kill his child. As a loving father, he can dismiss more easily the thought of killing his daughter, viewing it as an irrational idea or an illness. Ambivalence toward parenthood, however, is more realistic and therefore more threatening to his self-respect and basic values. This can be one way obsessions work: To prevent a psychologically painful idea from surfacing into your consciousness, you focus on another painful yet less disturbing idea.

People's psychological makeup can also influence the persistence of obsessions. Most of us have experienced a fleeting fear of losing control, such as accidentally dropping an infant or stepping in front of a train. Yet, we tend to dismiss it as an irrational momentary thought, and we reassure ourselves that everyone has such fleeting thoughts. Therefore, we don't pay attention to them; usually we don't even remember them. But if you are vulnerable psychologically, such thoughts can take on a significant meaning. For instance, if you are prone to guilt or shame, or have little trust in your self-control, such thoughts become threatening. You begin to wonder why you had the thoughts and what they mean. You start to worry that you are losing control, and you become extremely anxious. Now a vicious cycle begins. The more scared you become about the obsessive thought, the more you try to fight it. And as we mentioned earlier, by fighting it you reinforce its powerful persistence.

Low self-esteem can also play a role. If you regard yourself in high esteem, you are better prepared to withstand the consequences of your mistakes. You don't perceive mistakes as disastrous, and, therefore, you don't need to work so hard to prevent them. However, if your self-esteem is low, you are likely to become devastated by your own mistakes and work much harder to prevent them in the future. Your increased effort at thinking about how to protect yourself will encourage your obsessive worries.

It is often the case in medicine and in psychology that we know much more about how to cure a problem than about what causes it. While experts are searching vigorously for the cause of OCD, it is still considered an enigma. In contrast, it is much easier to understand how your problem persists once it has started. And fortunately that is all you need to understand in order to get better. After years of research, experts developed powerful and reliable techniques to diminish obsessive-compulsive symptoms. We will explain in Part II and Part III how you can apply these self-help skills to overcome your OCD symptoms.

2 🍒

THE LIVES OF OBSESSIVE-COMPULSIVES

SO OFTEN THE symptoms of obsessive-compulsive disorder can be compounded by isolation, embarrassment, and a feeling that no one understands your troubles. Have you ever thought, "I'm probably the only one in the world who has these kinds of problems"? Or, "No one could possibly be as troubled as me"? The truth is you are not alone; there are many other people who experience OCD symptoms. Learning more about them is an important first step in understanding how to change them.

In this chapter we will offer you a closer look at how each of the seven major types of OCD is developed and maintained. For each type, we will illustrate some of the ways the particular symptoms have developed in other people's lives. We will also include a chart that summarizes four primary aspects of that form of OCD: the typical situations that cause the distress or the urge to ritualize and that many sufferers try to avoid; thoughts, images, or impulses that cause distress; consequences that might occur if certain situations are not avoided or certain rituals are not performed; and compulsions you might develop if you have these fears.

27

Read the sections of this chapter that pertain to your types of symptoms, whether they are washing and cleaning, checking, repeating, ordering, hoarding, thinking rituals, or pure obsessions. This information will ready you for Chapter 3: Preparing for Your Self-Help Program.

Washers and Cleaners

For fifteen years, Libby's entire life had been controlled by her fears. It all started in the spring of 1973. One morning, as she prepared to feed her four pet hamsters, she discovered one had died during the night. Naturally she wondered why it had died.

"Maybe he died of rabies," she thought. "If he died of rabies, that means everyone who played with him may have rabies." Pretty soon Libby began to believe that the sewing room where the hamsters lived was contaminated with rabies germs. Because of her fear she decided that nothing in that room could be touched. To protect herself and others, she locked the door to the room and would allow no one to enter.

By locking the door, Libby believed she prevented rabies contamination from spreading to other areas of her home, and for several months she forgot about the problem. Then one day in early winter, as she was preparing a fire in her living room fireplace, she noticed that the chimney was blocked. She later discovered a dead squirrel there. Libby quickly concluded that the squirrel died of rabies. From then on, in her mind, the living room was contaminated by rabies. Even though the maid cleaned and scrubbed the entire room and its furniture, Libby would not sit by the fireplace, nor allow her husband to be near it.

Soon her fear of rabies spread to every outdoor animal. Libby first refused to walk in any wooded areas because a raccoon sitting above her in a tree might drop saliva directly into her mouth. The saliva would then enter her bloodstream and give her rabies.

Then her fears spread to parks, gardens, and even to her own cat. She was afraid that when the cat played outside, a squirrel might scratch him, he would contract rabies, and then pass it on to her and her family. So eventually, heartbroken, she had to give her cat away.

Libby's fear became so pervasive that even on hot summer days she wore pantyhose and shoes while she was out walking. In this way, she felt she was protecting herself from rabies germs entering her body through scratches on her legs.

This fear was her primary concern for ten years. Then, in 1983, Libby's mother was diagnosed with cancer, and she became obsessed with a fear of developing cancer through contact with her mother. Despite her worries, Libby continued to take care of her mother during the several months prior to her death.

After her mother died, Libby felt that all the clothes that she wore while tending to her mother were contaminated with cancer, and she threw them away. She also felt that all the objects inherited from her mother were contaminated. Items that were too valuable to be thrown away, such as sterling silverware, were relegated to a corner of the basement.

Two years prior to entering treatment Libby developed yet another obsession: She became consumed with fear of AIDS. She could no longer go to her usual flower shop because she thought the man running the store had AIDS.

Even her trusted hairdresser was no longer safe, because she suspected he too had AIDS. She immediately began to investigate the other hairdressers in town with the hope of discovering an uncontaminated beauty salon. Eventually she decided that hairdressers who were married and had children didn't have AIDS. But just in case she had guessed wrong, Libby never used a toilet at the hairdresser's.

Any time Libby entered her house after being outside, she

would wash herself extensively. Her showers, which lasted from an hour to an hour and a half, involved scrubbing every inch of her body, starting with her legs and ending with her scalp. And when her husband returned from fishing trips, she required that he decontaminate himself by washing and scrubbing according to her directions.

When she finally entered treatment, Libby suffered from all three of her primary obsessions relating to catching a disease. Each of the three fears—rabies, cancer, and AIDS—required several weeks of therapy, consisting of three treatment sessions per week. By the end of treatment, Libby was completely free of symptoms. She rarely felt the urge to wash, she enjoyed her walks in the woods and parks, and she used her mother's silverware without hesitation.

Libby's compulsive behavior is one of the most common in obsessive-compulsives, the washing-and-cleaning ritual. People with this obsession believe they will become "contaminated" or "dirty" from contact with certain situations or objects. If such contact is made, they may experience an unpleasant sensation directly on their skin. And they want nothing more than to get rid of this sensation.

Common contamination obsessions involve bodily secretions, such as feces, urine, menstrual blood, and sweat. In many cases, these worries involve the idea that bodily secretions are contaminated by germs and therefore should be avoided. For instance, some people fear that contact with public toilets will expose them to some disease that they, in turn, will transmit to others. Some may not have a particular disease in mind—only a vague sense of danger. While the actual chance of contracting disease in this manner is very low, the obsessive-compulsive feels and acts as if a disease is imminent.

The desire to avoid contact with germs is understandable. For instance, suppose you feel that dogs spread dangerous germs that can easily be transmitted to humans. It would be natural for you to begin avoiding dogs because you don't want to catch the illnesses that the dogs spread. Nor do you want to pass those germs on to those around you, such as your small children.

But obsessive-compulsives cannot successfully steer away from germs by simply avoiding dogs. One of the most prominent characteristics of this disorder is the belief that contamination can travel endlessly from one object to another even without physical contact. Imagine that you have developed concerns regarding contamination by dogs. Not only will you avoid dogs, but you will also avoid houses where dogs live, streets where dogs walk, parks where dogs roam. The chain of situations can become endless, and the entire physical world around you can become contaminated. It then becomes impossible to avoid dog germs by simply avoiding certain places. Therefore, you will create some active procedure to remove the contamination: You begin to wash.

COMMON FEATURES OF WASHERS AND CLEANERS:

Situations That Cause Distress or Urge to Ritualize and Tend to Be Avoided
- Anything that might contain "germs," e.g., public toilets, garbage.
- Anything that might feel "contaminated," e.g., a relative, one's hometown.
- Anything that feels "dirty," e.g., feces, urine, menstrual blood, sweat, the floor.
- Anything that might be a health hazard, e.g., chemicals, asbestos.

Thoughts, Images, Impulses That Provoke Distress
- "I am contaminated."
- "I'll be contaminated."
- "If I touch that, I'll certainly become dirty."
- "I'm not certain I have washed enough."

Feared Consequences of Not Avoiding or Ritualizing
- "I or someone else will become contaminated and will make things unsafe."
- "I or someone else will become ill or die."
- "I will be anxious forever."
- "I will lose my mind and go crazy."

Common Compulsions
- Hand washing
- Showering or bathing
- Changing clothes and washing them
- Cleaning surfaces or objects

You wash yourself, you wash your children, you urge your husband or wife to wash. That is the only way you can restore a sense of cleanliness and safety. Yet, even washing does not help for long, because as careful as you are, you inadvertently touch contaminated things. And your children are definitely not careful enough. Visitors come to your home contaminated by germs and in turn contaminate your home. So you start to clean everything in the house that might be contaminated. Over and over again you wash, scrub, disinfect throughout the house in order to maintain a clean, safe environment. Through this description of what actually happens to washers, you can see how some obsessive-compulsives become consumed with washing and cleaning rituals as the only way they can maintain some sense of safety.

Other fears of contamination are completely unrelated to germs or disease. Consider the case of Geraldine, who didn't actually fear germs and did not imagine any disasters that might ensue from her contamination. Geraldine's problem began when she was six months pregnant with her second child. During a visit one day, Geraldine's mother placed her hand on her daughter's belly and said, "My, the baby is growing up." Instantly, Geraldine felt contaminated and dirty, especially on the spot her mother had touched.

Within two months, her sense of contamination spread dramatically. Not only did she avoid her mother, but also anything that could be contaminated by her. She believed the mail was contaminated because deliveries came from a single post office where all the pieces were mixed together. Since her mail might have touched her mother's mail, she thought the letters she received were tainted by her mother's touch.

Money was also a problem. Because it passed among endless numbers of people, Geraldine could never be sure her money hadn't been in contact at some point with her mother. So she washed all her money with Lysol. As a result of this cleaning process, paper bills faded and looked fake. She had so much trouble with merchants that she had to pay for most purchases with well-washed coins.

Even more troublesome, one of her mother's neighbors worked at the same factory as Geraldine's husband, Bob. So to Geraldine the factory was contaminated, and so was her husband. In order to save her marriage, Geraldine constructed an elaborate daily routine. Every day before he left work, Bob called home so Geraldine could prepare for him. When he arrived, she would open the gate and the front door for him so that the handles would not become "unclean." Bob would go directly to the basement, take off his contaminated clothes, bathe, put his "dirty" clothes in the washer, and in the nude would climb the stairs where his wife waited with uncontaminated fresh clothes. From that moment, Bob was "clean" and was allowed into the house.

For six years Geraldine did not meet with her mother in person. Even when they talked on the phone she felt contaminated, as though contamination could travel through the phone lines. Therefore, before calling she first took off all her clothes and sat nude in a chair. This way, although her body and the chair became contaminated, she would be ready to take a cleansing bath as soon as the conversation ended.

These tedious habits continued until Geraldine sought treatment for her disorder. With enormous determination and a strong commitment, she rid herself of this problem within ten days. Today, eleven years after treatment, she continues to be symptom free. She has a normal relationship with her mother and now has only faded memories of her long struggle.

Like Geraldine, Susan did not fear disease or germs. Instead, she feared contamination by anything associated with her hometown. When Susan entered treatment she was thirty-two years old and had not seen her mother, siblings, or any other relatives for six years. This was because they lived in that hometown, which was the source of the contamination in her mind. In fact, she even avoided contact with relatives who lived in other cities because they occasionally met with her hometown family.

The problem began when Susan was thirteen. One Christmas Eve she climbed into the attic to find the tree ornaments. While there, she suddenly was struck by a strong sense of contamination. The attic, the objects in it, and especially those ornaments became "dirty." Soon the entire house was contaminated—and then the neighborhood. Susan became obsessed with washing and cleaning herself and her house. She prevented her family from entering her bedroom so that she could have a safe place in which to retreat. For Geraldine, contamination felt like strong, unpleasant sensations on her skin. Susan, however, described her contaminated feeling as a deep depression enveloping her, accompanied by pain in her chest. This pain and deep sadness were so distressing that Susan needed to wash and clean continuously in order to restore her emotional balance.

At eighteen, Susan left town to attend college. Once away from home, she viewed her entire hometown as contaminated, including all the people and objects in it. For instance, she thought coats produced in the town coat factory were contaminated, so clothing stores in any city selling the hometown brand were contaminated. These problems became worse after she married and had her first child, even though she continued to live in another city. In her mind her daughter's playmates were potentially contaminated because they might have bought clothes in stores that carried the hometown label. Like other washers, Susan believed that contamination could spread by indirect contact, so all clothes in those stores became contaminated. There was also a cereal company in her hometown, so all supermarkets carrying that brand of cereal provoked her fear.

In order to be able to buy food, Susan developed an intricate routine. In each store she identified where the cereal was shelved, then limited her purchases to items far from that aisle. These restrictions forced her to shop in many supermarkets in order to complete a week's shopping list.

Susan's life revolved around worrying, washing, and cleaning for six long years before she entered treatment. After treatment she let go of all her rituals and returned to a normal life and a productive job. She could comfortably visit her hometown and her parents. These changes have remained consistent throughout the eight years since treatment.

Checkers

At the time he entered treatment, David was twenty-seven, an accountant who was married with one young child. His obsessive-compulsive problems had developed when he was a teenager. In high school he was overly concerned about his assignments. He used to read a passage from a book over and over to make sure he comprehended it. He would go over his essays repeatedly in search of mistakes. For David, correcting an essay did not mean simply checking through a few times for sentence structure and grammatical errors. Instead, he pains-takingly reviewed every line dozens of times before moving on to the next line. He was obsessed with producing the "perfect" essay.

After David married and bought a home, his checking rit-uals began to spread and become more intense. He felt over-whelmed by even the most mundane responsibilities. He would check the stove and electrical appliances again and again before leaving home or going to bed. He'd check the lock on each window and door six to eight times. He was afraid the house would burn down or a burglar would break in if he didn't successfully complete all his rituals.

Over time David developed additional fears and correspond-ing rituals. The fear of harming others permeated almost every action he took. While driving he was afraid he'd unknowingly hit a pedestrian. If he drove over a bump in the road, he imag-ined it was a person's body and felt compelled to return and check. He feared the injured person would be lying in the middle of the road, bleeding to death. To prevent such a hor-rible possibility he avoided driving alone whenever possible. When he had to drive alone David would retrace his entire route, searching for the injured person. While checking for the injured person, David would imagine hitting another bump and believe he had hit the body a second time—or injured a new person. By imagining that this dreaded horror had actually happened, David was in a state of terror throughout his search.

After two to three hours, he would stop checking the road, not from satisfaction but from physical and emotional fatigue. Exhausted by his intense emotions, he would finally tear him-self away from the ordeal and drive home while trying to convince himself that nothing terrible had happened. But the terror would not end there. Upon parking the car in the drive-way, he would check his wheels for traces of blood. And the next day he would search the newspaper and listen to the radio for reports of a hit-and-run accident.

David's fear of hitting people while driving generalized to an overwhelming fear of accidentally killing any living thing. Before flushing the toilet, for instance, he would check for organisms crawling on the bowl or floating in the water to ensure that he wouldn't drown them. Even taking a walk became an arduous task. If he thought he'd stepped on a bug, he'd retrace his steps to search for the insect.

The disorder affected David's relationship with his toddler daughter. He began to fear that while carrying his daughter over a concrete floor he would accidentally drop her and cause her death. As a result, David was careful to carry her only across soft rugs, never hard floors. Since he was also terrified that his daughter would fall down the stairs, he would check the safety gate to the basement dozens of times a day to make sure it was closed.

By the time he entered treatment, David was spending five to six hours a day moving from one worry to another, checking things repeatedly in an attempt to prevent disasters. The common thread to all of his activities was his dread of hurting any living creature. The thought of killing a fly terrified him as much as the thought of killing his daughter.

David was involved in a brief, intensive treatment program like the one described in Chapter 7. Today, eight years later, he continues to enjoy the freedom he gained in treatment. He only has some minor concerns, which result in about ten minutes of checking rituals a day, mostly around securing the doors and windows of his home.

This second large group of obsessive-compulsives are those who, like David, repeatedly check things in order to forestall catastrophes. One way checkers differ from washers is in the reason for the compulsion. Many people who compulsively wash do so in order to remove the contamination and restore a sense of physical and emotional comfort. All checkers, however, are driven by their need to prevent disasters they fear will happen.

The most common feared disasters for checkers involve their physical environment. One might check the locks on windows and doors so that a burglar will not break in and kill the children and one's spouse. Or one might feel compelled to check the faucets throughout the house to prevent leaks from turning into floods, or check the appliances repeatedly to make sure the house won't catch on fire. The checker believes that such potential disasters would be entirely his or her fault since he neglected to check properly.

Disasters can be emotional as well as physical, such as to be scrutinized, looked down upon, or criticized by others. Richard, for instance, feared that when signing checks, he would inadvertently write, "I'm a fraud." In actuality he was not a fraud. He could never think about instances of dishonest activities nor did he ever have thoughts of deceiving other people on purpose. However, he was terrified he might humiliate himself by making a mistake that would suggest he was a fraud.

Consequently, when Richard signed his name to a check, he felt compelled to read the check over again and again. It took great effort for him to put the check into an envelope and seal it. Even after sealing it he felt compelled to open the envelope and verify his signature. He spent hours doing this every day, trying to write checks and often never being able to send them. Payment for bills was delayed for months while Richard struggled with this task.

Many checking rituals are an exaggeration of normal behavior. People often worry about locking doors and windows—most of us check our doors once before we go to bed at night. But obsessive-compulsive checkers exaggerate the possibility of something bad happening if they are not extremely careful ("someone will certainly break in and kill my family"). They also exaggerate how awful the consequence will be ("it is terrible to be criticized by my boss"). Because of this exaggeration, checkers become terrified with the idea that they might not have checked sufficiently ("did I really check the stove carefully?").

COMMON FEATURES OF CHECKERS:

Situations That Cause Distress or Urge to Ritualize and Tend to Be Avoided
- Making a mistake, e.g., writing the wrong amount on a check or misspelling a word.
- Any situation that might cause harm to oneself or to others such as:
- Leaving home without ensuring that the doors and windows are locked.
- Eating food without checking for harmful objects.
- Driving a car near pedestrians without checking for possibly hitting a person.
- Leaving home without unplugging electrical appliances.
- Leaving the medicine cabinet unlocked.

Thoughts, Images, Impulses That Provoke Distress
- "Did I check all the windows?"
- "Did I give too many pills to my sick child?"
- "Did I put on the brake in my car?"
- "Did I run over someone with my car?"
- "There might be a piece of glass in the food."

Feared Consequences of Not Avoiding or Ritualizing
- "Something terrible will happen."
- "Someone will break into the house, rob me, and harm my family."
- "My home will burn down."
- "My loved ones will be hurt or die."
- "I will be criticized, ridiculed, or humiliated."

Common Compulsions
- Repeated checking of doors, windows, car brakes, faucets, electrical appliances.

- Repeated checking of letters or forms before they are sent.
- Checking driving routes.
- Retracing one's activities mentally (mental checking).

Sometimes checking compulsions can be so extreme that the person becomes eccentric. Mary felt compelled to check things compulsively from the minute she got up in the morning until she went to sleep at night. Her greatest fear was that someone nearby might need help and she would not find out in time. For example, she constantly worried that there were neglected babies nearby who would die unless she was able to locate them. When she went shopping at a mall, she checked and double-checked for babies behind doors, in hallways, and in garbage cans, knowing somewhere in the back of her mind that she wouldn't really find any babies.

Mary's obsessions were not limited to babies. When she took walks through the woods, every shadow looked like a person lying on the ground. She then had to approach that shadow spot to ensure it was not a person. Momentarily convinced, she'd walk away. But several steps later, she had to return to the shadow and check again.

The pervasive doubt—did I check enough?—is often incapacitating. Mary would check a closet thoroughly, verifying that there were no babies. But a minute later she would begin to doubt, thinking "Maybe I didn't check it enough. I'd better go back and make sure no babies are in the closet." This is the same way the checker who worries that someone will break into his or her house will check the front door by turning the handle and shaking it repeatedly, concluding that the door is locked. But after taking a few steps toward the car, doubt sets in: "Did I really check it? Is it really locked?" This repetitious checking and doubting may look as if something is wrong with the checker's memory. However, psychological studies do not find general memory problems in obsessive-compulsives.

Rather, the difficulty to remember arises only during their checking behavior. The exaggerated concern with the consequences of an unlocked door causes high anxiety, which seems to interfere with memory.

Checkers are burdened with an extreme sense of responsibility and fear that they will not meet that responsibility. Therefore, at home they will compulsively check doors, windows, or the stove in order to protect their family. Yet, if they are spending the night at someone else's house, they don't feel compelled to check. This is because the responsibility for ensuring safety is the homeowner's, not theirs.

Repeaters

Paul grew up in a Catholic family that was quite involved in church activities. He served as an altar boy, followed the teachings of the church closely, and attended mass and confession regularly. Paul was underdeveloped physically as a child and adolescent. He was small in stature and, because of an early hormone deficiency, his body did not develop in the normal way. His classmates' teasing compounded his own sense of inadequacy. Yet, he always remained committed to his religious faith.

Paul's OC problem began at about age eighteen. One day as he was leaving church after Mass, an image of himself knocking over the statue of the Virgin Mary flashed in his mind. The image was quite vivid, even though it lasted for only a moment. Considering this image a blasphemy, Paul became extremely frightened that God would punish him for it.

As time passed, the image of himself knocking over the Virgin Mary's statue, and sometimes the image of the statue smashed on the ground, came more and more frequently. And he became more afraid of God's punishment. He felt shame and guilt, especially when images flashed uncontrollably across his mind during Mass. He was so distracted that he couldn't concentrate during the service.

Paul discovered that if he repeated over and over again the actions he engaged in while having the image, his anxiety and shame would be alleviated. For reasons not known to him, sequences of four repetitions became especially helpful. The process was not a simple one, however. In order for his actions to reduce his distress, even temporarily, he had to repeat them in a prescribed manner. For example, if the image of knocking over the statue entered his mind while brushing his hair he would have to brush his hair with his left hand in four short strokes on the top, the back, and each side of his head. If this sequence was disrupted, Paul would have to start all over again. And through the entire sequence he could not have a single image of the Virgin Mary's statue. If he did, he had to repeat the whole process again. In addition to repeating actions, Paul also had a thinking ritual: He prayed for forgiveness in a highly structured and rigid manner. Prayers, too, were repeated in sequences of fours, with an exact intonation and pauses.

Despite becoming consumed with his obsessions and compulsions, Paul continued with his education, through college and law school. By the time he entered treatment, he was working as a lawyer but enjoying little success in his career. At least some of his professional limitations were caused by his disorder. Throughout the day, he spent seven to eight hours either on attempts to fight the images of knocking over the Virgin Mary's statue or on his praying rituals.

Repeaters, like washers and checkers, use repetition of a particular action to ward off feared disasters. However, unlike checkers and washers, repeaters do not make a logical connection between their obsession and their ritual. Consider washing rituals: If you are distressed because of germs on your skin, or around you, it is logical that you would wash or clean the germs off. With checking rituals, if you are afraid someone is going to break into your house, you will want to make certain the windows and doors are locked. The rituals of repeaters, on the other hand, have magical rather than logical power.

COMMON FEATURES OF REPEATERS:

Situations That Cause Distress or Urge to Ritualize and Tend to Be Avoided
(Often there is no external situation that creates the distress.)
- Repeating an action the "wrong" number of times.
- Leaving the room and entering another room.
- Doing things the "wrong" way.

Thoughts, Images, Impulses That Provoke Distress
Any thought or image that produces anxiety, shame, guilt, or disgust, such as:
- "My husband will have an accident."
- "My neighbor is a nasty person."
- "I may utter mean things."
- "My parents will die."
- "My daughter will fail in school."
- "She [a friend] is a mean person."
- "I am a sinful person."

Feared Consequences of Not Avoiding or Ritualizing
- "Some unspecified disaster will occur."
- "Some unspecified harm will come to me or those I love."
- "I will be punished."
- "Bad luck will befall me or someone else."
- "Everybody will hate and despise me."

Common Compulsions
- Repeating an action until it feels "right."
- Repeating an action until the "bad" thought disappears.

Nancy, for instance, dressed and undressed hundreds of times a day, in a specific order, starting with her socks and moving upward to her shirt. The trigger for these compulsions was the thought that her husband or daughter might be in an accident. In order to protect them from being killed she had to dress and undress until the thought disappeared. Like most other obsessive-compulsives, when asked what the chances were that her husband and daughter would actually be killed if she didn't perform the ritual, Nancy would reply, "I know logically it doesn't make sense, but at the same time it feels as though it works." Even without a logical connection, the tie between the obsession and the compulsion for repeaters is the same as for checkers and some washers: The compulsions are performed in order to prevent some future catastrophe from occurring.

Orderers

Sarah, a thirty-five-year-old woman, felt compelled to arrange everything in her house. She had to place all objects in the closets in special ways. Shirts had to hang in a certain sequence and at a particular angle. Every time her children used their drawers or clothes, Sarah became extremely distressed. She spent all day going from one room to the next, rearranging anything which was disturbed. In addition, she had to make sure the bedspread was perfectly placed on each bed. If there was a single wrinkle, it had to be redone, sometimes requiring an hour's effort.

Another of her ordering compulsions involved placing pills, papers, and pencils into very complex patterns. The pills, for instance, were laid out on a table in the shape of flowers where all family members could see them. If someone touched a pill, she got very upset and arranged them again. This process could take hours. Maintaining symmetry was important too.

Each time she had to take a pill, Sarah reshaped the pattern so that the left and right sides matched.

Orderers often feel compelled to place objects in special patterns. For most orderers, the purpose of the rituals and their underlying logic are vague. Most are not driven by the need to prevent something terrible from happening. Instead, the need is often for perfection: "to set matters right."

Common Features of Orderers:

Situations That Cause Distress or Urge to Ritualize
- Objects not being placed in an exact order or sequence, e.g., bed sheets, clothes, pills, pencils, or papers.
- Someone else touching or rearranging such objects.
- Things being asymmetrical.
- Things being imperfect.

Thoughts, Images, Impulses That Provoke Distress
- "Things are out of place."
- "Things are touching each other in the wrong way."
- "The bedspread is wrinkled."

Feared Consequences of Not Avoiding or Ritualizing
- "I will be extremely distressed unless I rearrange things in the right way."
- More rarely: "Bad luck will happen if things are not in the right order."

Common Compulsions
- Arranging objects in one's environment "just right."
- Ordering objects in symmetry or according to certain rules.

If you were to ask orderers how they chose a particular order, they could not describe any logical process. It simply "feels right" compared to any other order. But this need for order is not like the average person's need to straighten up his or her desk. It is not like the mother who sees a chaotic mess in her teenager's bedroom and demands a more pleasing order. The true orderer has such a rigid sense of uniformity that moving an object even half an inch from its proper place causes a great deal of disturbance. This distress will not go away until the object is back in its place, half an inch to the right or left. For some, ordering rituals have the magical protective quality found in repeating behaviors. Such orderers may think, for example, "If I put things in a perfect order in this room, everything will be fine with my grandmother."

Hoarders

Hoarders are people who collect objects that most people would perceive as insignificant, and have tremendous difficulty throwing them away, for fear that someday they will need them. We all have some junk we know we'll never use, but "just in case," we keep it in the basement. Hoarding becomes a problem when the need to collect and sort things begins to control daily living, and when collections become so enormous that living space is sacrificed.

Unlike washers, checkers, or repeaters, most hoarders don't complain about their behavior and seem willing to live among their collections. Since they don't struggle with their problem, hoarders choose treatment less often than do others with OCD. But their families may become fed up with their overflowing collections and urge them to seek treatment.

Blanche came to our clinic for several consultations over a two-year period. Her husband, Peter, had hoarded for thirty years. She was desperate because Peter's compulsion increasingly controlled their lives. They were forced to rent a second apartment to house his collection of newspapers, pieces of paper he picked up in the street, and receipts for everything he'd bought for the past thirty years. When the second apartment became full, Peter's problems began to impose upon the family's apartment. First he filled the garage, then one bedroom, then another bedroom. Pretty soon the family's entire apartment was full of his collections, and he stubbornly resisted demands to throw anything away. When Blanche threw out some stacks, Peter became extremely upset and went to the garbage dump to retrieve them.

Peter did not seek treatment because he did not think his behavior was unreasonable. He knew his wife was bothered, but he believed that if she would simply ignore the piles, all would be well. In his mind, the collections represented an eccentricity, just like the eccentricities most people have.

Hoarders often do not experience the discomfort about their compulsions that other OC's feel. Washers and checkers become disturbed when contemplating future catastrophes. They also worry about their compulsive rituals. A washer doesn't like to scrub his or her hands all day. Similarly, a checker doesn't like standing in the kitchen for forty-five minutes to verify that the stove is off. Washers and checkers would rather not act as they do.

The typical hoarder, in contrast, doesn't resist the urge to collect. However, a hoarder who is forced to get rid of his collection feels the same anxiety experienced by thwarted washers and checkers. Such distress stems from his fear that certain things won't be there at the moment he needs them.

COMMON FEATURES OF HOARDERS:

Situations That Cause Distress or Urge to Ritualize
- Throwing things away.
- Someone else rearranging one's "collections."
- Leaving behind something that may later be needed.

Thoughts, Images, Impulses That Provoke Distress
- "What if I need this thing one day and I can't find it?"

- "What if I were to need this thing and I had thrown it away?"

Feared Consequences of Not Avoiding or Ritualizing
- "I won't be able to find something I need."
- "I won't be able to have something I need."

Common Compulsions
- Collecting useless items.
- Ordering "collections" in certain ways.

If a relationship with another person has great value to the hoarder, and if the hoarding compulsion threatens the continuation of that relationship, treatment for hoarding can be successful. One patient, Donna, hoarded a variety of objects, including newspapers, magazines, and paperback books. She would even search through the trash of other homes for papers. Donna did not allow anyone into her apartment for fear that her collections would be disturbed. In the past, when she allowed visitors into her apartment, they always messed up her delicate order. She would then have to spend hours restoring that order. Donna's boyfriend eventually found her problem intolerable and threatened to end their relationship if she didn't change her ways. This threat motivated her to seek treatment, and she then overcame her obsessive-compulsive hoarding.

Thinking Ritualizers, Worriers, and Pure Obsessionals

Thinking ritualizers, worriers, and pure obsessionals differ from other OC's in that they do not share clear-cut behavioral rituals. Their symptoms are similar; therefore, we will describe them in one section. One feature distinguishes the two groups: Pure obsessionals attempt to reduce the obsessional distress by using internal arguments; thinking ritualizers feel compelled to perform specific and exact mental routines in order to get relief from the obsessional thoughts.

THINKING RITUALIZERS The types of OCD we have described thus far can be identified by their observable behaviors: washing and cleaning, checking, repeating actions, creating order, and hoarding certain items. Some rituals, however, involve the repetition of thoughts or images instead of actions.

Bob, a thinking ritualizer, was deeply afraid of offending other people or being rude in conversation. Whenever he thought he had been impolite, he began to feel guilty and inadequate. To counteract this distress, he instituted an elaborate thinking process. First, after a conversation, he replayed the scene in his mind. A harsh self-critic, he would reprimand himself for hurting someone's feelings because he didn't smile enough or wasn't polite enough or didn't pay enough attention to the other person's feelings. Or perhaps he was in a rush and cut the person off in mid-sentence. Any such behaviors would stimulate Bob's self-criticism and cause him great distress. To reduce this distress, he prayed to God for forgiveness. In the beginning, Bob simply acted like an overly self-critical person. But later on the manner in which he prayed became highly ritualized, thus distinguishing him as an obsessive-compulsive.

Bob developed a specific set of prayers he mentally recited in a special order, with an exact tone and emphasis for each word. There was also a precise punctuation pattern, including a special pause after each sentence. If he made a mistake in the sequence, stumbled on a word in his mind, used the wrong punctuation, or didn't pause long enough, he had to begin again. Bob spent many hours praying in order to ward off the thought that he was a bad person who upset other people.

Thinking rituals such as praying or counting are quite common and often accompany behavioral rituals like Paul's repetition of actions (see the section Repeaters, page 41). Other OC's generate long mental lists of tasks they must perform and will repeatedly recall the lists for fear they will forget one task. Still others will form a mental image of how they have checked each door and window. They review that mental picture again and again, trying to remember every detail of the action. In this way they attempt to ward off their doubt and their need to actually check things. The purpose of thinking rituals and behavioral rituals are the same. Both are performed in order to reduce distress and to restore a sense of safety.

WORRIERS AND PURE OBSESSIONALS Worriers and pure obsessionals experience a form of internal dialogue close to that of thinking ritualizers. One negative thought will rise up to consciousness and produce distress. A reassuring thought will then rise up to diminish that discomfort. Such dialogues are common in all of us. However, for pure obsessionals they are carried to the extreme and become controlling and uncontrollable.

Don was a Vietnam veteran who constantly obsessed about a companion's death in battle. He believed he could have saved his friend if he had taken the correct action. While obsessing, he first visually reviewed the event, including how the bomb dropped near him and hit his friend. Then he reprimanded himself for not being more helpful. At this point, a second voice in him would say, "Nobody else could have done better. You did the best you could." This reassuring voice gave him short-term relief. But the first voice returned, saying, "Oh, no, you didn't do the best you could. You know you could have saved him." This internal battle would continue for hours at a time, and eventually it cost him his job.

Although no compulsive rituals are involved in an obsessional dialogue, it contains a basic OCD dynamic. The first voice, harshly critical, reflects an obsession, since it produces distress. The second voice, reassuring, amounts to a compulsion, as its purpose is to reduce the distress. The only component missing is the *precise* nature of the typical compulsive ritual. The exact content can change each episode—this is also what distinguishes the pure obsessional from the thinking ritualizer.

The pattern of worriers and pure obsessionals may involve concern with future disasters as well as guilt and remorse about the past. Some obsessionals suffer from guilt-provoking impulses or images. Common is an image of killing a loved one, such as using a knife to slaughter one's spouse or child. A voice then arises, saying, "A person who imagines such things is likely to act upon them." The reassuring voice then says, "No, you're not going to act on that. You're not crazy. You have a good heart; you'd never do that." "How do I know I'll never do it? Maybe I will," replies the obsessive voice. On and on this mentally exhausting dialogue will go until finally the obsession fades away, only to return several hours later.

COMMON FEATURES OF THINKING RITUALIZERS, WORRIERS, AND PURE OBSESSIONALS:

Situations That Cause Distress or Urge to Ritualize and Tend to Be Avoided
- Any situation in which someone could be harmed.
- Any situation in which an OC could make a "bad" mistake.
- Any place that provokes distressing thoughts.

Thoughts, Images, Impulses, That Provoke Distress
- Harsh self-criticism or criticism of others.
- The thought of having made a mistake or done something wrong.
- Guilt or remorse about the past.
- Thoughts of some future unpleasant experience.
- Thoughts or images of harming or killing someone.

- Thoughts of committing an immoral or sexually perverse act.
- Blurting out an insult or obscenity.
- Doing something embarrassing.
- Acting on a criminal impulse.

Feared Consequences of Not Avoiding or Ritualizing
- "I will fail."
- "I will be punished."
- "Something terrible will happen."
- "Bad luck will come upon me."
- "I will accidentally hurt or kill someone."
- "I will be sinful."
- "I will lose control and go crazy."
- "I will be humiliated."
- "My distress will never go away, and I will always be terribly upset."

Common Thinking Compulsions
- Praying to oneself.
- Counting to oneself.
- Making mental lists.
- Retracing activities in memory.
- Mentally repeating phrases, e.g., "God is good."

Obsessions about harming someone are exemplified by Joel, a thirty-two-year-old man who was an accomplished and well-respected architect. At the time his OC symptoms first appeared, he had been happily married for two years and was the proud father of a one-year-old girl. One night Joel was home taking care of his daughter. As he watched the child sleep in the crib, he suddenly had the impulse to kill her.

Joel then began to panic: His heart raced, he became dizzy, his legs became weak, and he started shaking. The impulses continued through the night, robbing him of his sleep. After that night, Joel experienced the impulse to kill his daughter forty to fifty times a day. He would say to himself, "Oh, my God, how can I have these thoughts? If I allow these thoughts to continue, they might take on a life of their own, and I will kill my daughter. Therefore, I have to stop them from entering my mind." He feared that if the urges continued like this, he would lose control of them sooner or later and act on them, even though the thought of losing his daughter was unbearably painful.

As we discussed in Chapter 1, the more you fight an obsession, the more frequent and intense it becomes. This is called a paradoxical effect, something we all experience at times. For instance, if someone commands you, "Do not think of a red elephant," you will automatically respond by thinking about a red elephant. And so it was with Joel. His attempt to banish the impulse actually worsened his problem. He would command himself, "Don't think about killing her"—then he could think of nothing else.

Joel's distress intensified after hearing a story on the radio about a schizophrenic woman who killed her children. This story convinced him that he too could kill his daughter. Over the next year and a half, Joel's problem progressively worsened. And every time he heard about a murder, it reinforced his belief that he would eventually kill his daughter. He also developed the impulse to kill himself. Driving in the car, for instance, he would suddenly feel compelled to turn the car toward the edge of the bridge he was crossing. But these thoughts were not as powerful as those of killing his daughter.

Once Joel learned of cognitive-behavioral treatment, he became determined to conquer his problem. The turning point in his therapy was his willingness to accept his impulses rather than trying to push them away, thus reversing the paradoxical effects that make obsessions so intense. We will further discuss this reversal process in Chapter 4. And in Chapter 10, Joel will explain to you what he did to overcome his obsessions.

3 ❦

Preparing for Your Self-Help Program

IF YOU SUFFER from persistent worries or compulsive behaviors, you are painfully aware how tedious and exhausting your symptoms can be. You know about the futile attempts to fight the distressing thoughts via senseless behaviors, only to gain moments of relief. You know that the whole cycle will soon start again, and still you cannot stop it.

Being so involved with your problem, it may not be easy for you to step back and analyze it objectively. However, this chapter is designed to help you put your OC symptoms in perspective. The step-by-step approach outlined here is taken from a specialized treatment program for obsessions and compulsions that has been developed and perfected over the last twenty years.

Worries and Obsessions

Your obsessions can be divided into three parts. The first part is the distress you feel when you confront certain situations or objects. The second is the thoughts, images, or impulses that provoke your distress, anxiety, or shame. The third is what you fear will happen if you don't protect yourself or others by ritualizing, repeating words or numbers, avoiding certain situations, or somehow fighting the obsession.

For example, the following are specific situations that have been known to cause distress: If you are a worrier, you may become anxious each night your teenage daughter goes out on a date. If you are a checker, perhaps you get upset as you walk away from the front door on your way to work or when you leave electrical appliances plugged in or hit a bump while driving a car. If you are a washer, you may become bothered after using a public toilet or after handling furniture wax or bug spray, picking things up from the floor, or touching a doorknob in a public building. If you are a hoarder, you might feel extremely distressed when leaving behind a useless piece of paper on the street.

Now, think about what concerns and worries you. Write down ten to fifteen situations or objects that cause you the greatest distress, anxiety, or shame, situations that provoke your strongest urge to ritualize. Once you've done that, look at Table 1, which follows. You will notice that there are numbers on the right side. These represent the degree of distress you feel when you confront a situation or object. The distress scale ranges from 0 to 100. On this scale, 0 indicates that being in the situation, touching the object, or being near it does not distress you at all. The number 100 means that the situation is the most distressing that you could ever imagine and would create enormous anxiety or distress in you. On this imaginary scale, you will rate each situation somewhere between 0 and 100. Situations producing only mild anxiety can be rated as low as 10 or 20. If you can imagine yourself moderately distressed, you would rate the situation as about 50. If you think you would be highly anxious, rate the situation as 70 or 80.

TABLE 1:
SITUATIONS THAT CAUSE ME DISTRESS, ANXIETY, OR URGE TO
RITUALIZE

	Degree of Distress (0–100)*
1. _____	about 50
2. _____	about 60
3. _____	about 70
4. _____	about 70
5. _____	about 80
6. _____	about 80
7. _____	about 90
8. _____	about 90
9. _____	about 95
10. _____	about 100

* 0 = no distress; 100 = highest-possible distress

Now transfer to Table 1 situations from your list that provoke at least moderate discomfort, situations you would rate
as about 50 on the scale. Continuing down the list, include the
situations or objects that produce the level of distress indicated
in the right column. For example, if you are a checker and you
cannot drive without rechecking your route again and again,
consider how anxious you would be if you were driving in the
middle of a busy street with many pedestrians and without
checking your rearview mirror. If this situation is the most
distressing you could imagine, write it in the space designated
as about 100. Driving on a deserted country road may cause
only moderate distress. If so, write it in the space designated as
about 50. Note up to ten situations in this way. It is not
necessary to fill in all ten spaces.

Some people do not get distressed by actual situations or objects. Their distress is always caused by thoughts, images, or impulses. If your OCD problem is of this kind, skip Table 1 and begin with Table 2.

The second component of obsessions concerns the thoughts, images, or impulses that provoke your distress, anxiety, and shame. Examples of these types of thoughts and impulses are the impulse to harm yourself by driving into a tree; the thought "I am contaminated"; or the thought "Did I lock the front door of my home?" Considering them is not an easy task, so take your time to reflect on the obsessive thoughts that have entered your mind most frequently in the last week or two. Use Table 2 (page 58), and list these obsessions in the designated spaces. In doing so, follow the same instructions given for Table 1.

The third part of an obsession is what you fear *will happen* if you *don't* protect yourself or others by ritualizing, repeating words or numbers, avoiding certain situations, or somehow fighting the obsessions. If you are worried about an exam, perhaps you fear that if you don't continue anxiously repeating the facts, you will forget the most important material to be covered. If you are a checker, you may worry that you might allow a burglar into your home to take your possessions and harm your family, all because you didn't make sure the doors and windows were properly locked. Or perhaps you obsess about your house burning down because you failed to check the stove or the electrical appliances. If you are a repeater, you might worry that if you neglect to repeat actions, numbers, or words in a certain way, you or your loved ones might be involved in a serious accident.

If you are a washer, you might be worried about using household chemicals, having some on your hands, then cooking without properly cleaning your hands, and thus causing illness to those who eat your food. Or you may worry that you have used the toilet without washing your hands suffi-

TABLE 2:
THOUGHTS, IMAGES, OR IMPULSES THAT PROVOKE MY DISTRESS

	Degree of Distress (0–100)*
1. _____	about 50
2. _____	about 70
3. _____	about 80
4. _____	about 90
5. _____	about 90
6. _____	about 100

*0 = no distress; 100 = highest-possible distress

ciently, and consequently you will be ill or cause others to be ill.

Some OC's don't worry about a specific future disaster. They just worry that they will be extremely uncomfortable unless they wash, clean, check, or order. Others fear that something bad will happen but do not know exactly what it will be.

Think about what you fear will happen if you do not engage in your ritualistic action or thought. List these fears on Table 3, which follows. As you write your feared consequences, note that there are two types. The first include consequences that come from external situations, such as failure on a test, a burglary if a door is not properly locked, or getting a disease from touching an object. The second include consequences caused by your thoughts or impulses, such as "I will accidentally stab my child," "I will lose control and go crazy," or "My distress will never go away, and I will always be terribly upset." Choose consequences that provoke 50 to 100 on your distress scale, and write them on Table 3. Write a number from 50 to 100 next to each worry indicating how much it distresses you.

Now we want you to make another judgment about each

TABLE 3:
FEARED CONSEQUENCES OF NOT AVOIDING OR RITUALIZING

	*How Much It Distresses Me (50–100)**	*How Much I Believe This Will Really Happen (0–100)†*
A. Consequences from External Situations		
1. _____	_____	_____
2. _____	_____	_____
3. _____	_____	_____
4. _____	_____	_____
B. Consequences Caused by My Thoughts or Impulses		
1. _____	_____	_____
2. _____	_____	_____
3. _____	_____	_____
4. _____	_____	_____

* 50 = moderate distress; 100 = highest-possible distress;   †0 = don't believe it will happen; 100 = will definitely happen

consequence. Rate how much *you believe* each feared consequence *will come true* if you stop ritualizing or fighting the obsession. It is important that as you make this judgment you stay calm and think as rationally as you can how much you believe your fears will *actually* come true. Think with your head, not with your fear. Use a scale from 0 to 100. Zero means "I don't really believe it will happen, even though I am very much afraid of it." A rating of 100 means "I definitely believe, beyond any doubt, that it will happen."

You may have noticed that there are specific objects, situations, thoughts, or activities you avoid. Many washers who are concerned with germs avoid using public bathrooms. For instance, David, who was described in Chapter 2, avoided driving alone or carrying his daughter on concrete floors. Orderers might avoid inviting guests home because they might disrupt their order. And the person who is afraid he might stab his daughter will hide all kitchen knives.

What are the situations you avoid in order to gain some sense of safety? List such situations, objects, thoughts, or activities on Table 4 (page 61). Beside each item, rate how often you avoid it, using a scale from 0 to 100. A zero means "I never avoid it." A 100 means "I always completely avoid it." Of course, as with all other scales, there are points in between. If you avoid a situation 50 percent of the time, write 50 next to it, and so on. This exercise will help you identify the situations you tend to avoid and help you plan your self-help program in Chapter 7.

How to Analyze Your Compulsions

You have now learned a lot more about your worries and obsessions by just organizing them according to their various components. Next, we will address your compulsions, which we also call rituals. On Table 5 (page 62), you will find a list of ritualistic behaviors and thoughts. Place a check mark next to each of the compulsions you perform. Now rank the rituals you marked by placing a *1* beside your most-frequent ritual, a 2 next to your second-most-frequent ritual, and so forth.

Starting with the ritual that occupies most of your time, describe the most common action you perform within this ritual, and estimate how much time you spend during a typical day with it. For example, if you are a washer, how many times

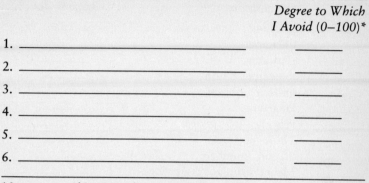

TABLE 4:
SITUATIONS I AVOID IN ORDER TO FEEL SAFE

	Degree to Which I Avoid (0–100)*
1. _____	_____
2. _____	_____
3. _____	_____
4. _____	_____
5. _____	_____
6. _____	_____

* 0 = never avoid it; 100 = always completely avoid it

do you wash your hands during the day? How long does each hand washing take? Do you wash just your hands, or do you wash your arms as well? How many showers do you take? How long are they? What detergents do you use? If you are a cleaner, what are the objects you tend to clean most? How much time do you spend cleaning your clothes? Other people's clothes? Furniture? Floors, sinks, toilets? If you are a checker, list what you tend to check most, such as doors, windows, electrical appliances, specific lights in the house or office, your car, the route you have just driven, your checkbook, or written forms.

If you are an orderer, describe exactly what you order. Do you straighten the bed for a long time? Do you straighten clothes? Pictures? Other objects around the house? Drawers? Do you organize things in symmetry?

In later chapters you will use the information from this form as you design your self-help program. It will help you in deciding what characteristics of your rituals you can modify and which of your rituals to face first.

TABLE 5:
BEHAVIORAL AND COGNITIVE COMPULSIONS

	Compulsion	Rank Order
_____	Washing	_____
_____	Cleaning	_____
_____	Checking	_____
_____	Repeating actions	_____
_____	Ordering objects	_____
_____	Hoarding	_____
_____	Praying	_____
_____	Thinking rituals	_____
_____	"Good" numbers	_____
_____	Mental listing or reviewing	_____
_____	Other	_____

Common Actions of My Ritual	*Amount of Time Spent Daily*
Ritual #1: _____	_____
Action: _____	
_____	
Ritual #2: _____	_____
Action: _____	
_____	
Ritual #3: _____	_____
Action: _____	
_____	
Ritual #4: _____	_____
Action: _____	
_____	

Distinguishing Obsessions and Compulsions from Other Psychological Problems

Now, begin to think about the relationship between your obsessions and your compulsions. Do you engage in rituals such as washing your hands to reduce your concern with illness in order to decrease your obsessional distress? Or do you repeat actions such as tapping on the table or rubbing your head over and over again without having any idea of why you perform them. Your answer to these questions is very important.

This self-help program is especially designed for people who feel that their worries and obsessions are exaggerated and unwanted and that their compulsions and avoidances are intended to decrease their distress. If you do not recognize that your ritualistic behavior directly protects you from being overwhelmed with distress, and if your compulsions are purely automatic, then we suggest that you consult a mental-health professional for guidance. A trained mental-health specialist can help you determine whether your symptoms reflect some psychological problem other than OCD.

Sufferers of several other mental disorders may also engage in repeated rigid sequences of actions. Those suffering from schizophrenia, for instance, often present repeated actions, like moving their hands in a specific manner, or walking with a stiff, rigid gait. People with organic disorders, like brain damage or mental retardation, may also show such stereotyped movements. But the compulsive actions of the OC sufferer *are* distinct from those other repeated actions. In OCD the compulsive action has the purpose of neutralizing some obsessional thought or image and is aimed directly at reducing obsessional distress or preventing a future catastrophe.

Ritualizing individuals with other kinds of psychological problems will not usually have a logical explanation. Only OC's will have an explanation that connects the obsessions and compulsions—they are suffering from repetitive unpleasant thoughts (obsessions) and use the repetitive behaviors (compulsions) to feel better.

Compulsions are also distinct from excessive habits like overeating, nail biting, or pulling out hairs from the head, known as trichotillomania. In these behaviors, there is no specific distress, guilt, or shame that the compulsive behaviors are designed to counterbalance. There is no expected catastrophic consequence if the person resists the urge to engage in the nervous habit.

Overeaters, for instance, may feel a general buildup of tension. They start to think about food and begin to have an urge to eat. They resist going to the refrigerator but finally give in and binge. Binging gives them relief from their stress, even though they might then begin to feel guilt or shame or regret the consequences of overeating.

OC's, unlike overeaters, do not simply engage in a compulsion to get relief from a *general* tension. They suffer from quite *specific* distress from which they seek relief, and they often fear *specific* consequences of not ritualizing, such as "If I don't wash, I will be contaminated and get ill" or "If I don't check, then the house will burn down." Again, the compulsions are directly related to relieving the distress of the obsession or preventing the feared consequences from happening.

Another diagnosis that is sometimes confused with OCD is the obsessive-compulsive personality. All of us have met people who constantly strive for perfection, who have strict and often unattainable standards, who pay extreme attention to details, follow a rigid life pattern, and have difficulty deviating from it. People who have obsessive-compulsive personalities are overconcerned with cleanliness and order and go to great lengths to avoid mistakes. It would appear that the personality style of these individuals would be related to OCD. In fact, some people with OCD are also considered obsessive-compulsive personalities. Others are not. Thus, not every neat, orderly person is an OCD sufferer.

At the same time, not all OC's are neat and organized. For instance, if you walk into the home of an obsessive-compulsive washer, you might actually encounter chaos and dirt. This is because the person is so consumed with ritualizing and worrying about contamination that he doesn't have time to engage in the normal organization or cleaning of his surroundings. Many washers, like Robin from the introduction, refrain from cleaning their home for fear that they will spread contamination throughout.

At this point we want to emphasize again that most OC's are able to recognize that both their obsessions and compulsions are largely senseless. Although they spend a lot of energy worrying about possible catastrophes and trying to protect themselves and others from harm, they are aware that their obsessions are produced in their own mind and are not imposed on them by an external force. They know that their compulsions are of their own doing, even though they do not feel in control of them. Most recognize that their obsessions and compulsions don't truly make sense, and they attempt to resist them.

A psychological problem often found in people with OCD is depression. It is not surprising that individuals whose lives become consumed by obsessive thoughts and incessant repetitive behaviors become depressed. In most cases, the person experiences depression as a reaction to his OC symptoms, and it usually lifts after successful treatment of the OCD.

In some cases depression develops first. For these individuals, obsessions and ruminations are usually part of a depressive disorder. Depressed people see themselves as defective and unworthy. They perceive the world around them as negative and devoid of pleasure. And they imagine the problems and frustrations they feel today as never ending. In their mind, tomorrow will be just as bad as today. Their obsessive thoughts tend to reflect these themes: "I'm an unworthy person," "I'll never feel better," "Nobody likes me, and why should they?"

If you are depressed, you may lack the energy or motivation to follow your self-help program alone. One option is to seek out a friend who can support you and assist you with your practice. A second option is to consult a mental-health professional for help with your depression before you begin the Initial Self-Help Program or during the program. Also, if you do not actually have OCD, a professional can direct you to the most appropriate treatment for your problem.

Should You Seek Professional Help?

Now that you have analyzed your symptoms and made sure you indeed have obsessions and compulsions, you are in a position to decide whether you should use the self-help program on your own or with the guidance of a mental-health professional. Look back over your answers to Tables 1–5 in this chapter. Did you rate several items on Tables 1 and 2 as "about 90" or "about 100"? On Table 3, did you rate any item in the far-right column as close to 100, indicating that you firmly believe such a consequence will actually happen? Now look at your responses on Table 5. Add up the total number of hours you spend each day on your rituals. Do you also spend much time obsessing during the day? Add that amount to the time you spend on your rituals. Is it more than two hours?

These answers will help you decide. If you suffer from *severe* symptoms (Tables 1 and 2) and *firmly* believe that some of your most distressing fears will come true (Table 3) and you spend *two or more hours per day* ritualizing (Table 5) or obsessing, we encourage you to seek guidance from a mental-health professional who specializes in OCD. This expert will further evaluate you and help you follow this self-help program. We suggest this because of your severe symptoms, which continually intrude in your day. Severe symptoms are more difficult to overcome on your own.

Which Self-Help Program Should You Use?

You are now ready to begin your self-help program. Regardless of whether you begin alone, with a supportive friend, or with a mental-health professional, everyone should start with the Initial Self-Help Program described in the next three chapters. It is designed for all sufferers of OCD and will be the only program needed for people with *worries* and *obsessions*.

If you also suffer from compulsions, practice the skills of the Initial Self-Help Program, described in Chapter 5, *persistently* on a *daily* basis for several weeks. If you find you are improving, then you can stick with this approach. However, if after a few weeks you find that you are not continuing to improve or that the suggestions of this program are not helping you control your symptoms, move on to Part III of this book, the Intensive Three-Week Program.

PART II

The Initial Self-Help Program

4 ❦

Meeting the
Challenges

In this chapter, we will clarify the essential changes you need to make in your thoughts and attitudes before you can get rid of your obsessive-compulsive symptoms. Such changes will prepare you for the specific self-help skills outlined for you in the coming chapters.

One characteristic of OC symptoms is that they can be extremely persistent over time. The diagram on page 72 illustrates how this persistence occurs in someone who has both obsessions and compulsions. First, some event that stimulates your obsession occurs. This event can be something in your environment, such as noticing a light switch in your home or a doorknob at a store entrance. Or it might be simply a passing thought. It's this event that triggers your obsessive thought, image, or impulse.

Once you begin obsessing, you become distressed and anxious. Since obsessions tend to stay on your mind, you remain distressed for a long time. This state is extremely unpleasant, and naturally you want to stop it. In the past you have discovered you can decrease the obsessional distress by engaging in some compulsive action. Therefore, your strong wish to find

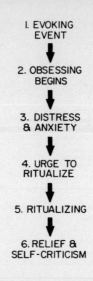

I. EVOKING
EVENT

2. OBSESSING
BEGINS

3. DISTRESS
& ANXIETY

4. URGE TO
RITUALIZE

5. RITUALIZING

6. RELIEF &
SELF-CRITICISM

THE SEQUENCE OF OCD SYMPTOMS

relief causes you to feel an urge to ritualize. You then follow through on this urge by actually ritualizing—that is, you begin to engage in washing, repeating, checking, etc. Sometimes you also try to resist the compulsive behavior, since it, by itself, is quite distressing.

After ritualizing, you will usually experience some relief from the obsessional discomfort. This relief, unfortunately, is only temporary, and soon another event will begin the cycle again. Nonetheless, the pattern becomes set, because ritualizing is the only way you have discovered that brings you some relief. At the end of each cycle, you feel discouraged, disappointed, and self-critical—once again you have become stuck in this irrational pattern.

All treatments of OC symptoms, whether by professionals or self-help, aim to break this vicious cyclic pattern. In the next two chapters we will demonstrate how you can apply some basic therapeutic principles to break this pattern and to begin to bring your symptoms under control.

The Four Challenges

There are four challenges you must face as you start to control your symptoms:

CHALLENGE 1: BECOME DETERMINED TO CONQUER YOUR PROBLEM You must decide that now is the right time for you to make the changes necessary to conquer your OC symptoms. First, you must believe that you have the right to be well. These symptoms have troubled you and intruded in your life for far too long. You are a worthy person, deserving of comfort, success, and peace. Therefore, you are ready to do whatever it takes to put your life back together.

Second, you need to believe that you can overcome your OC problem. Remember that this is possible, that other people with problems similar to yours have improved, and that you too can change. We will help strengthen this belief by introducing you throughout the book to other sufferers who have overcome their problem.

As you follow the suggestions offered, you will need to take the risk of experimenting with options that are completely different from your current obsessive-compulsive practices. For instance, so far you have chosen to worry over and over again about particular fearful events. Some of you have also repeated thoughts or behaviors to prevent any disasters from occurring. We will ask you to gradually change these thoughts and behaviors, to not worry in the way you have been accustomed to and to shift the way you perform your rituals. Taking the risk of giving up your old ways and trying new behaviors will require faith in this new process and a lot of courage, because when we try something new we are never sure it will work. That's where your determination comes in. It will help you to persist through short-term doubts, uncertainties, and discomfort in order to heal yourself. Your determination will help you through disappointments and difficulties that may arise during your self-help program.

CHALLENGE 2: GAIN THE PERSPECTIVE THAT YOUR WORRIES ARE IRRATIONAL Keep in mind that OCD is considered an anxiety disorder. This is because it is based on anxious preoccupation with *unrealistic* concerns. Yet, the obsessions are so powerful and so disturbing that you become overwhelmed by them, believe they represent true threats, and become preoccupied with how to protect yourself and others.

When you dread passing on deadly germs, killing your own child, or causing a terrible accident, these are compelling fears. How can you believe that these concerns are not based on reality? And such beliefs will tend to intensify your symptoms. We are asking you to adopt a new belief: Your obsessional concerns are highly exaggerated.

Now, granted, it is extremely difficult to think rationally when we are horrified. So, it won't be surprising that even after you gain perspective about your obsessions, during the moments of obsessing you will still sometimes believe that your fears are real. Through self-help skills we will help you learn that your beliefs are unfounded. By continuing to strengthen this perspective, when you face your obsessions in the future, you will be better able to respond to them in a new way.

CHALLENGE 3: CONSIDER THAT RITUALIZING IS NOT THE ONLY WAY TO REDUCE YOUR DISTRESS Most OC's believe that if they don't ritualize, they will remain distressed forever. It is no wonder that they continue to ritualize to ensure some measure of comfort. If you share this belief, you must be willing to challenge it in order to discover that there are other ways to reduce your distress. It will be extremely difficult to give up your compulsions unless you are willing to experiment with new behaviors. Such experimenting requires that you first consider that other options might work. Once again, willingness to change your actions will require your courage, since your compulsions have worked for you in the past.

CHALLENGE 4: ACCEPT YOUR OBSESSIONS INSTEAD OF RE-SISTING THEM This is, by far, the most difficult challenge. On the surface it seems to contradict Challenge 1. If we are asking you to believe that your worries are irrational, why should you also accept them? It doesn't seem logical. And you are right. We spoke in Chapter 1 about the use of paradox: choices that seem the *opposite* of logic. This is one of those times when a paradoxical shift in your thinking will greatly influence how much your obsessions will bother you. And when they don't bother you as much, you will naturally not dwell on them as much. So even though you need to accept that your obsessions are unrealistic, you need to simultaneously *accept* that you are having them. When you master this challenge, you'll be surprised at the results!

Let's look more closely at this process. If you are like most OC's, you probably are aware of how much you try to resist your obsessions. Since you have experienced the psychological pain of getting stuck in your obsessions, you become afraid of them and try to avoid them by any means. Yet, research has shown that attempts to resist thoughts usually make them more likely to persist.

The more you resist your obsessions, the longer they remain in your mind and the more frequently they return. It is as though your attempts to solve your problem actually worsen it.

If this is true, then by accepting your obsessions, they should diminish. That is what often happens when people choose to face their worries directly, even to encourage them: The painful thoughts begin to fade away. It's like cutting off the fuel to a fire. Your obsessions will continue to be powerful as long as you remain afraid of them and fight them. When you stop resisting, they will no longer persist.

Logically you may understand this idea. Yet, the only way you will truly have confidence in this principle is by putting it into practice. This is why you need to accept the challenge of courage: We will ask you to practice skills that you fear might increase your suffering rather than give you relief.

Of course, no one really wants to have obsessions, and the purpose of treatment is to get rid of them. Yet, the approach that we propose is paradoxical; it dictates that you act in a way that at first glance seems illogical. The paradoxical position we encourage you to take is: "In order to get rid of my obsessional thoughts, I am willing to accept them." Whenever you first notice yourself obsessing, respond by accepting that this in fact is what's occurring.

Accepting your worries will require that you develop a new and different inner voice to respond to them. Instead of saying, "I can't let myself start obsessing now, it would be *awful*," you take the position, "It's OK for me to be obsessing right now."

Starting to Change the Pattern

Your symptoms do not exist in a vacuum. They depend on a specific cyclical pattern of thoughts, actions, and reactions. If you can keep your obsessions from leading directly into your compulsive behaviors and if you can reduce your distress and anxiety, you can prevent your typical pattern from occurring. There is no need to make a direct frontal attack on your irrational obsessions. Instead of directly, anxiously attempting to rid yourself of them, we will ask you to change the manner in which you respond to them.

By accepting the four challenges, you will begin to change the pattern (see Table 6). The strength of your obsessions and compulsions will decrease when you become determined to conquer your symptoms, when you remind yourself of the unrealistic nature of your worries, and when you are willing to consider new options other than rituals for reducing your distress.

Challenge 4, accepting your obsessions instead of resisting them, will constitute the first step in changing your pattern. This is the first place for you to start practicing your self-help skills. Anytime you begin to obsess, permit the obsession to exist at that moment. Work toward not fighting the obsession and not being critical of yourself for having it. Your basic stance should be "It's OK to have that thought."

INTRODUCE A NEW ATTITUDE The statement "It is OK to have the obsessions" should not be simply subvocalized during times of trouble. Rather it should reflect a basic change in your attitude, and its effectiveness is conditional on your commitment to believe it. This means that once you notice yourself obsessing, you allow those thoughts to continue. As soon as you welcome them, you make the thoughts voluntary. If you accept them, you need not struggle to get rid of them. Therefore, by your acceptance, you reduce your compelling urge to ritualize.

We are not implying that this approach—accepting the obsessions while considering their content irrational—will instantly diminish them. If it were that easy, your symptoms would never have become so devastating. Yet this shift in attitude is the first important step toward your recovery. Choosing to accept your obsessions instead of fighting them is based on your decision not to take the content of the thoughts or images at face value (Challenge 2). By remembering that your specific worries are exaggerated, you are likely to prevent your anxiety from escalating.

TABLE 6:
ACCEPTING THE FOUR CHALLENGES

Problem Position	Self-Help Position
1. I will always be controlled by this problem.	1. I am now determined to conquer this problem.
2. I believe my obsessional concerns are accurate.	2. My obsessions are exaggerated and unrealistic.
3. The rituals are the only way to reduce my distress.	3. There are other options to reduce my distress.
4. I *must* stop my obsessions.	4. I accept my obsessions.

In the next chapter we will describe several approaches you can use to modify your worries and concerns. Then in Chapter 6, we will explain some techniques you can use to change your rituals while preparing yourself to give them up. As you decide to explore these options, there is one further attitude that will help your progress. You are about to dismantle a very powerful and longstanding fortress. And it takes patience to do so. You must not be quick to judge the worth or worthlessness of any particular technique, whether it aims to modify your attitudes, emotions, or behavior.

Dismissing an option prematurely, or becoming discouraged too soon about slow progress, will limit your success. People often view each encounter with their symptoms as a test of how well or how poorly they are doing and how able or unable they are to change. Yet, each time you view your experience as a test, you set yourself up for disappointment, discouragement, self-criticism, and resignation.

Instead, we encourage you to consider your experiences as practice. By doing so, you can evaluate what you have learned as well as identify what problems are more difficult and require additional attention. Most important, you will continue to be supportive of your own efforts and worth during the self-help program.

5 🍏

LETTING GO OF WORRIES AND OBSESSIONS

IN THIS CHAPTER we will address how to overcome your worries and obsessions. We will teach you new ways to act each time you notice yourself worrying. Then we will introduce four effective self-help techniques to practice during times when you are not worrying. These techniques will strengthen your ability to control your obsessions once they begin.

One note before getting started. In Chapter 1 we distinguished worries as anxiety-provoking thoughts about topics that can change from day to day. We defined obsessions as distressing thoughts, images, or impulses that recur again and again. The techniques described in this chapter will help both worrying and obsessing. Therefore, we will use these terms interchangeably.

What to Do During Obsessing

Now we are asking you to put Challenge 4 from Chapter 4 into play. When you begin to worry, you have two options. The first is to fight and resist the obsessions. This option, as you know, increases your distress and intensifies the obsessions, and until now, you have been responding in this way. We encourage you to try a different option: <u>Accept</u> the anxious thought. So even though your ultimate goal is to stop obsessing, the way to best *reach* that goal is to develop this attitude of acceptance: It's OK that I just had that thought, and it's OK if it returns.

Remember that obsessions are *involuntary* thoughts or images. If you choose to have them, by definition you increase your control over them. That in itself will be a significant change in your pattern, but it is only the first step. Once you accomplish this step, your next move should be to find more ways to bring your obsessions under your voluntary control without having to resist them. How do you achieve this goal? Here are two options to practice.

SELF-HELP OPTION 1: POSTPONE OBSESSING If you respond to your obsessions by attempting to get rid of them instantly, to have them gone *now* and *forever,* you will probably fail at the task. It's just too big a change to make. (You already

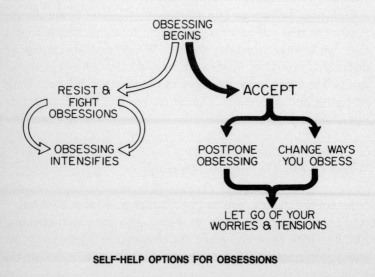

SELF-HELP OPTIONS FOR OBSESSIONS

know this is true because this has been your strategy in the past.) Instead, take a smaller, more manageable step in order to gain control of one more part of the obsessional process. Let yourself have the obsessions. Make a commitment to pay attention to your worries. Simply take control of *when* you do worry. The essence of this technique is to stall the obsessions. You decide not to ignore your worries. However, you are simply going to *postpone attending to them for a bit*.

This stalling tactic can help you gain control over your obsessions in two ways. First, by postponing your worries for a limited period, you don't get into the vicious cycle that stems from fighting them; rather you allow other momentary interests to replace the obsessions and occupy your attention. Time spent on these other interests may also diminish your chances of returning to the original obsessions. Second, even if the other interests don't continue to occupy your attention and you return to your original obsessions, you have broken your rigid pattern of becoming completely consumed with worry whenever an obsession enters your mind.

POSTPONING OBSESSING

1. Mentally agree to pay attention to the obsessions.
2. Choose a specific time in the future when you will return to them.
3. As that time arrives either start obsessing or consider postponing the obsessions to another specified time. Whenever possible, choose to postpone.

As you begin to practice this technique, try to postpone your obsessions for a few minutes only. Here is an example of how to implement the postponing technique: As you are sitting at your desk working, the thought "How will I be able to make all my payments this month?" enters your mind. This obsessive concern has been intruding into your working hours for the past several weeks. It is 9:00 A.M. You promise yourself that you will return in five minutes to the thought about how you will make ends meet. You set your timer for five minutes and return to your work. When the five minutes are over, you must make the next decision, to postpone the worry for another five minutes or to focus on it.

If postponing a second time is too difficult for you, designate a specific length of time you will permit yourself to worry. In this example, perhaps you decide to worry for five minutes if needed, then postpone again for five minutes, and so forth until you can completely let go of the worry. During your postponing time, be sure to refocus your attention on other activities that will hold your interest. Get back to your work, call a friend, or take a brisk walk. Don't wait idly for the time to pass.

Usually the longer you stall, the less powerful the obsessions will be. So whenever possible, choose to postpone again and again. Each day, gradually expand your postponing time until you are able to postpone up to several hours. Soon you will discover that when you return to that thought hours later, it simply doesn't trouble you as it did at first, and it will be much easier to just dismiss it.

SELF-HELP OPTION 2: CHANGE THE WAYS YOU OBSESS From time to time all of us experience an irrational worry or a moment's frightening image. These experiences are part of our mental life, and they have no great significance. Therefore, most of us can let go of such thoughts or images. If you expect to never have an obsessive moment in your life, you certainly are going to be disappointed.

A momentary obsession by itself is unimportant; it's how you react to it that creates the problem. Whenever you can, treat your obsession as if it was a momentary distressing experience. *Do not* analyze why you have experienced it, what it means, or whether you will be able to stop it. Since all obsessions are distressing, it is natural that you will have an initial negative reaction. Your task, however, is to let go of that initial reaction. Here are the steps to take:

CHANGING THE WAYS YOU OBSESS

1. Mentally step back and acknowledge that you have just started to obsess.
2. Notice your emotional response to the obsession. Are you anxious? Scared? Ashamed?
3. Remind yourself that it is OK to have a momentary obsession.
4. Reassure yourself at this moment that the obsessive content is irrational. Don't analyze.
5. Change your emotional response to the obsession by taking specific actions (i.e., writing down the obsession, singing it, changing the picture).

Let's look at how this process works. Consider the case of Sandra, a thirty-five-year-old woman who notices a lump in one of her breasts while taking a self-exam. She becomes concerned about what this new growth means and calls her physician for the earliest possible appointment. During her visit, Sandra's physician palpates the lump, orders a mammogram, and later is able to reassure Sandra that this lump is absolutely not cancerous. It is only a thickening of the glandular tissue, a fibroadenoma. Although logically she believes her doctor, time and again during the next several weeks she becomes stuck in worried thoughts about cancer.

Once Sandra decides that these thoughts are irrational and wants to stop them, here is what she says to herself: 1. "Oh, no, I've started worrying again about cancer." 2. "I really get terribly anxious every time I work myself up like this." 3. "It's OK that I just had that thought. After all, it was a pretty scary time until Dr. Patterson gave me the results." 4. "I know that actually I'm in good health and I don't really have cancer."

Then she closes her eyes and remembers sitting in the office as Dr. Patterson told her the good news. She creates the mental picture of her physician's face and hears the reassuring tone in her voice, then begins to relax. Before she opens her eyes, she also imagines a scene five years from today, sitting in that same office. She hears those identical comforting words and sees a smile on her own face. In this scene five years have passed, and she is healthy and strong. Feeling much more at ease now, she opens her eyes and returns to her activities.

Using imagery as Sandra did is only one of the ways you can change your emotional response to your obsessions. Here are three specific suggestions to help achieve this goal:

Write Down the Obsession. Carry a pencil and small pad of paper with you throughout the day. When you begin obsessing, write down your exact thoughts or a few phrases that describe your images or impulses. If you continue obsessing, write down your next thoughts, even if they duplicate what you have already written. When you obsess, you tend to repeat the same content again and again. When you write out the obsessions, you recognize how repetitive and senseless they are. This perspective weakens the obsessions. After a while you will probably experience the task of writing verbatim all the obsessional content as a chore. This way it becomes more work to obsess than to let it go. And the effort involved will discourage you from continuing to obsess.

Sing the Obsession. This technique can be used with obsessive thoughts but not with impulses or images. Pick up a short phrase that summarizes your obsession. Ignore its meaning for a while. Continue to repeat the words, but do so within a simple melody. At first glance, this idea may seem silly. Here you are, suffering from terribly distressing symptoms, and we ask you to hum a few bars. There is a purpose for doing this. The process of singing your obsessions makes it difficult to simultaneously stay distressed. Keep up this tune for a few minutes. Whenever you feel you are less emotionally involved with these thoughts, let go of the tune and the words. Turn your attention elsewhere.

Change the Picture. If your obsessions include a distressing image, you may find it helpful to consciously alter that mental picture or replace it with a new one before letting go of your emotions. For example, if you imagine your boss yelling at you, replace it with a picture of you and your boss having a pleasant conversation. If you imagine yourself dying of cancer, see yourself at 101 years old, smiling, rocking on your porch, surrounded by your family. If you have just imagined yourself slapping your child, picture yourself slowly, lovingly stroking the child's hair.

Or close your eyes and imagine your worry having some physical form. Place it on a cloud right in front of you. See the cloud begin to slowly float away. Imagine that the farther away the cloud floats, the smaller the obsession becomes and the more relaxed and comfortable you feel.

Make sure that as you see these new images, you also begin to shift from distressing feelings to pleasant ones. Choose images that will make you feel comfortable, relaxed, humored, or pleasant, so that they can replace your anxiety and worry.

Another useful approach is to replay the obsessional image but change the distorting, frightening components in some cartoonlike fashion. For example, if you are intimidated by your boss's criticism, see her about two feet tall and yourself next to her as your normal size. When she attempts to yell at you, see bubbles coming out of her mouth instead of words.

In this same way, if you have frightening repetitive images of stabbing someone with a knife or scissors, you can replay those images immediately after they occur. If a knife was used in your image, change the knife into Styrofoam and make it three feet long. If it was a pair of scissors, turn it into Silly Putty and see it drooping in your hand.

It may take a while before you can successfully apply this method to dislodge your obsessions. Some obsessions feel so strong that you will be unable to let go of them right away. Nonetheless, continue to practice this approach as a way to get some perspective on your irrational worries.

Letting Go of Your Worries and Tensions

Worries or obsessions do not usually continue uninterrupted twenty-four hours a day, seven days a week. Usually they come and go, depending on your daily activities—perhaps an intense business discussion, your children's demand for attention, or the exhaustion that leads to sleep will limit the time you obsess. Yet, the goal is for you to have greater control over how and when you stop obsessing.

Each of the two options—postponing or changing your obsessions—will help you gain a sense of mastery over your thoughts. They give you the chance to control certain aspects of your obsessions instead of being controlled by them. Each of them prepares you for the next stage, which is to *stop your worries and return to your daily activities*. If you look back at the diagram on page 80 you will see how the steps fit together. Once you notice you are worrying, stop for a moment and decide that it is OK to have the obsessive thoughts. Then select a way to modify the obsession—postpone it, change how you obsess, or both. It may take a few weeks of practicing accepting your obsessions and changing before you can let go of them altogether.

At this point you consciously choose to stop obsessing. Since most people become physically tense and anxious when they try to stop these thoughts, now you also practice letting go of those tensions. First you decide to stop the intrusive thoughts or images. Then you reinforce your decision with positive statements to yourself. Mentally support yourself by saying such things as "Now is not the time to think about it. I can think about it later." To reduce your anxiety, practice some brief relaxation techniques, such as those described on p. 90 and 91. Then shift your attention toward some new activity. Engage someone in conversation, go back to your work, or get involved with something that can keep you mentally busy. Go shopping; run two laps around your neighborhood; write a detailed letter to a friend. Don't create a void in your activities; that will simply give the worry an opportunity to creep back into your thoughts.

LETTING GO OF YOUR WORRIES AND TENSIONS

1. Decide to stop the intrusive thoughts or images.
2. Reinforce your decision with positive statements to yourself.
3. Practice some brief anxiety-reducing relaxation techniques.
4. Shift your attention toward a new activity.

Sometimes it's hard to shift your attention to a new topic. After all, most worries stay around because their content is so compelling. Have you ever tried to focus on reading a book or magazine as a way to distract yourself from worried thoughts? Remember sometimes how five minutes will go by and you are still reading the same paragraph? Let's look more closely at the two ways you can increase your chances of success at this point: actively reinforcing your decision to stop obsessing and reducing your physical tensions.

1. HOW TO USE POSITIVE STATEMENTS We have suggested that the first way to help yourself is to accept the fact that you

are obsessing. By doing this you don't anxiously resist your thoughts and thus they will not have such a strong hold on you. From this stance of acceptance, you then either postpone your obsessions or change them in some way, which further reduces the grip of worry. At this point, then, you have become less preoccupied with these thoughts, and they are less emotionally involving. Now you are ready to say good-bye to them. Do so by reminding yourself of your decision: These thoughts are exaggerated, and focusing on them now is not helpful. Whenever you feel drawn back into worried thoughts, think of a statement that supports your commitment. Literally subvocalize this statement, and help yourself *believe* your own words. Don't just mentally recite lines you don't hold to be true.

Here is a list of such positive statements. You can choose among these or use them as guides to create your own supportive words.

SUPPORTIVE STATEMENTS TO HELP END OBSESSIONS

- That thought isn't helpful right now.
- Now is not the time to think about it. I can think about it later.
- This is irrational. I'm going to let it go.
- I won't argue with an irrational thought.
- This is *not* an emergency. I can slow down and think clearly about what I need.
- This feels threatening and urgent, but it really isn't.
- I don't have to be perfect to be OK.
- I don't have to figure out this question. The best thing to do is just drop it.
- It's OK to make mistakes.
- I already know from my past experiences that these fears are irrational.
- I have to take risks in order to be free. I'm willing to take this risk.

- It's OK that I just had that thought/image, *and* it doesn't mean *anything*. I don't have to pay attention to it.
- I'm ready to move on now.
- I can handle being wrong.
- I don't deserve to suffer like this. I deserve to feel comfortable.
- That's not my responsibility.
- That's not my problem.
- I've done the best I can.
- It's good practice to let go of this worry. I want to practice.

Before you practice any of these options, be sure that you are really committed to getting rid of the particular worries you are addressing. Make this decision during a time when you are not in the throes of your obsessions—when you are feeling relatively calm and can gain perspective. If you wait until you are in the midst of an intense obsession, naturally you will be confused and uncertain about what to do. The content of the obsession will draw you into its spiral of anxiety and distress. At that time you don't want to be trying to make a decision like "Do I need to be worrying about this or not?" At that moment, in all likelihood you will remain indecisive. And your uncertainty will create an internal debate that deepens your trap, i.e., "I've got to stop these thoughts. But what if they are true?" It is as though your resisting statements give your fearful thoughts greater opportunity to grow.

So decide ahead of time not to analyze your choices in the middle of an obsession. Make sure this is a *firm* decision. Then choose an *automatic* response that reflects your position. For instance, you might decide that the next time you notice you've begun to worry, you will write down, verbatim, every thought that comes into your mind until you start repeating your statements. Then you will tell yourself, "I know these worries are irrational. I'm ready to move on now."

2. LET GO OF YOUR TENSIONS Even after you decide to stop your worried thinking and are able to shift your attention to some new activity, you will probably notice you are still physically tense. You can feel more comfortable and in control if you also let some of those tensions go. At other times you may feel so tense and anxious that you cannot concentrate on any self-help skills. You need a way to relax enough to take care of yourself.

Here are a couple of simple breathing techniques that promote physical relaxation. At first, practice them ten to fifteen times a day for several weeks. Use them during times of transition, such as right after you get off the telephone or while waiting in the car at a stoplight or when you've just finished with a file at work and are ready to begin another project. Of course they are especially useful in helping you let go of tension and become calm. When you need a strategy to help you let go of a worry, you can use these techniques.

The first technique, called the Calming Breath, requires about twenty seconds. It can be used when you want a quick, easy way to begin relaxing. If you usually experience a rapid heartbeat when you become anxious, this is a simple way to help slow your heart rate. Tension tends to build up in the body's muscles, so before or after you take this breath, you might want to literally shake your hands and arms and even each of your legs for a few seconds. When you do this, imagine you are shaking free from all those worried, uptight thoughts as well as loosening the tension from your muscles.

CALMING BREATH

1. Take a long, slow breath in through your nose, first filling your lower lungs, then your upper lungs.
2. Hold your breath to the count of three.
3. Exhale *slowly* through pursed lips while you relax the muscles in your face, jaw, shoulders, and stomach.

The second brief relaxation technique is called Calming Counts. It requires a little over a minute's time and offers two added benefits. First, it provides you with a longer opportunity to quiet your mind and body. Second, it is a good way to disrupt repetitious, unproductive thinking. If you decide to use Calming Counts, call time out on all other thinking and direct your full attention to this practice.

CALMING COUNTS

1. Take a long, deep breath and exhale it *slowly* while saying the word *relax* silently.
2. Close your eyes and imagine your body beginning to relax.
3. Let yourself take ten gentle, easy breaths. Count down, starting with *ten,* with each exhale. While you are breathing comfortably, notice any tensions, perhaps in your jaw or forehead or stomach. Imagine those tensions loosening.
4. When you reach *one,* open your eyes again.

Practice this once now, starting with a nice deep breath, the slow exhale, and the ten gentle breaths.

As you open your eyes and before you become active again, take a moment to mentally scan your body. What do you notice? Has anything changed? If you feel a pleasant heaviness, lightness, or tingling, or the sensation that some of your muscles have been able to "unwind," if your breathing feels calmer, then you are learning firsthand what it feels like to relax.

Did you have trouble keeping track of the numbers or become distracted by other thoughts? The better you can passively focus on the counting, the calmer your body and mind become. Yet, the harder you "work" at trying to focus, the harder this task becomes. Your job is *not* to focus intently on how your breathing is changing nor is it to judge how well or poorly you are performing this task. It is simply to let each exhale be a marker for the next number in your mind: inhale . . . exhale . . . ten . . . inhale . . . exhale . . . nine . . . and so forth. When some worrisome thought or image comes into your mind, gently dismiss it and return to the counting.

Before we move on, try Calming Counts once more, this time taking twenty breaths and counting each exhale, from twenty to one. Once again, notice how you feel as you finish.

If you are in the midst of worrying, Calming Counts will also serve as a postponing technique, as we discussed earlier in this chapter. In essence you say to your worries, "I'll be back to you in sixty seconds. First I'm going to take time to quiet down." Then devote *100 percent of your attention* for one minute to Calming Counts. If you can turn off your worries and also reduce your physical tension even for sixty seconds, then you will have a greater chance of getting some perspective on your irrational or exaggerated thoughts. You may also be ready to use some of the supportive statements we talked about, such as "This is *not* an emergency. I can slow down and think clearly about what I need."

These two techniques, Calming Breath and Calming Counts, are simple and straightforward. However, your ability to relax your body on cue in a brief time period may require some practice, especially since you want to use it during stressful moments. To learn more about developing these skills, refer to Dr. Reid Wilson's self-help book *Don't Panic: Taking Control of Anxiety Attacks* (Perennial Library).

Creating Structured Practice

So far we have described ways you can respond during worrying periods. Let's look at other techniques you can practice when you're *not* worrying. These four kinds of structured practice can help you gain control over your obsessions. Read through them, decide which might be helpful for you, and try them.

PRACTICE 1: SET ASIDE DAILY WORRY TIME If you are troubled by an obsession that tends to preoccupy your mind throughout the day, designate a specific "worry time" daily. This is another mental ploy that, like accepting your worry, is paradoxical. Instead of resisting your obsessions, you will choose periods during the day that you *purposely* devote to obsessing.

Set aside two specific ten- to fifteen-minute periods each day as your designated worry time. Treat this time as a special contemplative period. You should have no interruptions and no other tasks to disturb you. During this time focus solely on your worries by thinking of how bad things are or might become.

It is essential that you do not consider the bright side *at all*. Dwell on the bad, and don't try to stop your thoughts. Spend the entire time thinking of the negative. Repeat the same worry for the full ten to fifteen minutes. Don't make the mistake of saying, "Oh, well, I don't have many worried thoughts today. I'll just skip this practice time." Concentrate on becoming highly distressed as you focus on your obsessions. Continue this practice for a minimum of one week, even if the specific obsession is no longer bothersome.

DAILY WORRY TIME

1. Set aside two worry periods per day of ten to fifteen minutes each.
2. Spend this entire period worrying.
3. Do not think of any positive alternatives.
4. Do not try to convince yourself that your worries are irrational.
5. If necessary, repeat the same worries again and again until the worry time is over.
6. Try to become as distressed as possible while worrying.

People who have used this technique are surprised at how hard it is to fill a fifteen-minute period with worries. This is because typically when you obsess you struggle to think positively or to stop the worries. When you stop struggling and voluntarily choose to worry, an obsession that typically intruded throughout the day cannot sustain itself for even a quarter of an hour. Once again, it's hard to maintain an obsession unless you simultaneously resist it. So if you, too, run out of worries, that's a good sign! But continue for the full designated time, even if you have to repeat the same distressing thoughts.

The daily worry time will also help you to use the postponing technique more effectively. You will be more likely to stop obsessive thoughts and save them for your assigned time. Here's how they work together. When you use worry time daily, you will run out of worries during that period and will struggle with reviewing the same thoughts again and again. During other times of the day you will be more likely to catch yourself obsessing. You will tend to remember how difficult it was to obsess during the worry period and you will gradually develop the perspective needed for saying, "That thought will wait until five-fifteen. I'll have plenty of time for it then." Combining the postponing technique with a couple of daily worry times will increase your sense of control over your obsessions.

PRACTICE 2: LISTEN TO A LOOP TAPE OF YOUR OBSESSIONS If your obsessive thoughts take the form of a word, a group of words, a sentence, or block of sentences that is repeated again and again, you might benefit from the use of a loop tape. Loop tapes vary in length from ten seconds to three minutes and are often used to record outgoing messages on a telephone answering machine. When the tape is left running, it will play the same message continuously.

To practice this technique, write down the sentence or narrative exactly as it comes spontaneously into your mind. Then record it on an appropriate length of loop tape. Listen to the tape for forty-five minutes or longer each day. While listening to the tape, try to become as distressed as possible. Use the tape daily until the content of the message no longer distresses you. If after forty-five minutes your anxiety has not yet dropped, continue listening until your distress has decreased by at least 50 percent from its peak level. Even if your discomfort decreases within a few days, continue this practice for at least a week.

LOOP TAPE PRACTICE OF BRIEF OBSESSIONS

1. Write down the words, phrases, or sentences of obsessive thoughts exactly as they spontaneously come into your mind.
2. Depending on the length of time required for stating the complete message, record them on a ten-second to three-minute loop tape.
3. Listen to the loop tape daily for forty-five minutes or longer, attempting to become as distressed as possible by the message.
4. Continue practicing each day until your distress has decreased significantly.

This technique works on the principle called habituation, which we will discuss in detail in Chapter 7. It simply means that when one is confronted with the same distressing situation or thought repeatedly over a prolonged period of time, one's distress decreases. The time required for habituation may vary greatly depending on how strong your distress is. Strong distress requires more time to habituate. Therefore, we ask that you pay attention to how distressed you are and keep listening to the tape until you notice your distress decreasing significantly.

If you do not notice a significant improvement within a week, then you may want to reconsider the way in which you are applying this technique. For instance, are you actually listening to the tape when you play it, or are you thinking about other things? For the tape to work you have to immerse yourself completely in the taped message.

If you find that your mind is wandering, call it back. It is important that you continue to pay attention to the message. Just as you would not expect to learn from a lecture while you are daydreaming, you cannot learn new ways to relate to your obsessions if you are lost in irrelevant thoughts while the tape is playing.

For two years, Dale, a twenty-three-year-old woman, was consumed with the fear that she was a lesbian. Even though she experienced no homosexual desires and was not attracted to the gay life-style, she was worried she might be a lesbian. As is true for all obsessives, she loathed obsessing, yet felt no control over her thoughts. As Dale put it in her own words: "Life used to be a living hell. I was constantly obsessing. My fear was that I was gay. I turned the questions over and over again in my mind. Was I gay? Was I attracted to my sex or the opposite sex?—etc., etc. To say, 'Yes, I am gay,' was not an alternative. It meant panic. So I would continue asking the questions, and if they led me to answering, 'Yes,' I would have a panic attack."

Dale's first self-help practice was listening to a thirty-second loop tape on which she recorded her primary obsessive thoughts and questions: "Am I gay? What is my response to females? What if I get turned on? What is my response to men? Do I get turned on? If I don't, then I'm gay. If I think so much about being gay, I must be gay."

Dale listened to this loop tape one hour a day for five days in a row. In the first day's practice she was extremely anxious most of the time. During practice on the second day she felt quite sad, without understanding why. For the next three days, Dale could not conjure up distress while listening to the tape and had to struggle to focus attention on it. This five-day practice provided her with a perspective on the irrational nature of her obsessions. She could then let go of them when they spontaneously occurred during the day. She gradually came to believe that the content of her obsessions was meaningless, even though it was troublesome. Over time, the frequency of those obsessions decreased, occurring only during times when she was overly tired or mentally stressed.

PRACTICE 3: LISTEN TO AN AUDIOTAPE OF YOUR EXTENDED OBSESSIONS Remember Joel, from Chapter 2, who was afraid that his impulses to kill his young daughter would actually lead him to do so? Those impulsive thoughts struck terror in him, and he fought to rid them from his mind. As you know by now, fighting obsessional thoughts always increases, rather than decreases, their frequency and intensity.

Joel's desire to fight his frightening, shameful thoughts was natural, more so because he believed that struggling against the impulse to kill his daughter would prevent him from actually doing so. Giving up the struggle, he believed, would increase the likelihood that he would kill his daughter. Nevertheless, Joel was willing to try letting go of his struggle with the thought in order to help him control his obsession. Therefore, he practiced imagining again and again that he was killing his daughter. He wrote stories about how he would kill her and recorded these stories onto an audiotape, then listened to them for long periods of time.

You can imagine how painful it must have been for Joel to listen to the tapes during the first days, but he was willing to persist with the hope that this practice would help him. To produce this tape, Joel generated detailed descriptions of the following scenario: He is about to strangle his daughter. The girl is begging, "No, Daddy. No, Daddy." His wife is pleading with him to stop, and yet he continues because the impulse is stronger than he is. He finally kills the girl and his wife as well and is sent to prison.

At first, Joel could not generate these stories without breaking down into tears and he could only maintain the image for a short time. Gradually, though, he was able to think about the stories and listen to his voice on tape with relative calmness. It was only then that he could start letting go, allowing the impulses to enter his consciousness spontaneously without constantly fighting them.

Obsessions like Joel's are best treated with prolonged listening to an audio recording of the story. The process is as follows. Write out in detail the feared story so that it is four or five pages long. To create the text of the story, imagine you are in the middle of a spontaneous obsession. Don't describe how you obsess, such as, "When I lie in bed I start to think about how I will or will not kill myself." Instead, write a moment-by-moment description in the present tense using the exact words and pictures that appear in your mind. Describe all that you see, do, think, hear, and feel. Don't write your analysis of the experience. Simply describe it as if you are experiencing it right now.

For instance, if you obsess about your boss firing you, describe the setting. What is the boss wearing when he is doing the firing? In which room is this occurring? What are you wearing? What day and hour is it? Is it a nice or a dreary day? Where are you sitting and where is your boss sitting? How do you feel? Are you anxious? If so, how do you notice your feeling? Are you sweating? Is your mouth dry? Do you have knots in your stomach? All these details should be included in your tape. Most important are your reactions during the event. Pay attention to your bodily reactions when you imagine the worrisome event. Try to create enough text to produce stories that total twenty to forty-five minutes in length.

Read your story aloud several times to rehearse your tone and pacing. The purpose of the tape is to elicit in you the same emotions that you typically would have while obsessing. Practice reading your script in a way that helps you experience those emotions as strongly as possible. Then record the story on an appropriate-length audiotape. Each day listen repeatedly to this tape for forty-five minutes, longer if necessary. As you listen to the tape, imagine that the story is all really happening, and let yourself experience the distress evoked. The more you are in touch with your feelings while you listen, the more benefits you will gain from your practice.

A special process takes place when you hear your own voice describing your obsessions on tape. All of a sudden, instead of coming from inside your head, your obsessions are coming from a distance, as if someone else is experiencing them. Yet at the same time you know it is your own voice talking and your own obsessions being described. So it is as though the experience belongs to you on one level and doesn't belong to you on another. Therefore, the obsessional tape offers you a new perspective on your problem. This stepping-back process will help you break the spell.

Continue daily practice with one worry or obsession until it no longer elicits undue distress. If you practice in the right way, you should notice changes in your distress within five to seven days. Then make new tapes about other worries or obsessions that bother you, and follow the same process again.

As with the loop tape, your progress will be slower if you allow your mind to wander while you listen. If you are not noticing improvement, make sure you are doing all you can to respond to the recorded story as intensely as you would to an actual obsession.

Sometimes you may have trouble trying to identify the exact reasons why you are so anxious or distressed. An example is Jennifer, a woman who sought treatment for her obsession about a terminal illness. Jennifer was continuously preoccupied with this thought. She called doctors repeatedly and plied her medical-student husband with questions designed to alleviate her distress. Seeking reassurance, like any other ritual, provides temporary relief, but the worries and obsessions return sooner or later.

Initially, Jennifer presented her problem as fear of dying of rabies, and accordingly her treatment program included an extended tape recording that described how she actually came down with the disease and finally died. Jennifer became somewhat anxious at certain points during the practice but did not get as anxious as one might expect, given her extreme anxiety when thoughts about rabies occurred spontaneously. Nor did she become less fearful of dogs. After eight practice days with the tape, Jennifer did not experience any improvement. Puzzled by her lack of progress, the therapist decided to reanalyze the problem. It then became clear that it was the doubt about whether she had rabies rather than the dying itself that caused her distress. The knowledge that she was actually dying was less disturbing than being left in the dark with doubt.

With this insight, a new tape was prepared that focused on her uncertainty. Listening to this tape, Jennifer became extremely anxious. After four practices she began to get used to the message, and her anxiety lessened. After eight practices the obsession lost its power and subsided.

AUDIOTAPE PRACTICE OF AN EXTENDED OBSESSION

1. Write out a detailed story of the feared event in the following way:
   A. Imagine you are in the middle of a spontaneous obsession.
   B. Write a moment-by-moment description of the exact words and pictures that come into your mind.
   C. Give as many details as possible about the setting, your action, the responses of others, and especially your emotions.
2. Read your story aloud several times to rehearse the tone and pacing that best reflect your emotions within the story.
3. Record your story on an audiotape.
4. Each day listen repeatedly to the tape for forty-five minutes or longer. Attempt to become as distressed as possible by the story.
5. Continue daily practice until you no longer feel undue discomfort.
6. Repeat this process for each additional obsession.

PRACTICE 4: DIRECTLY FACE THE SITUATIONS YOU AVOID
The three structured practice techniques we have presented so far are based on a single principle: *To overcome a fear, you must approach the fear.* We have asked you to face your obsessions directly by either using designated worry time, listening to a loop tape, or listening to an extended audiotape of your obsession. Practice 4 carries this same principle to actual situations that you typically avoid because of your obsessions. Facing those situations directly for an extended period of time will be the only way for you to overcome all of your fears. If you avoid situations in order to feel safer, then you will need to practice this option.

Joel, for example, protected himself from killing his daughter by avoiding staying alone with her. He feared having a momentary lapse of control during which he might commit this horrible act. His program, then, included being alone with his daughter. As he became less anxious while listening to his tapes, he began to spend longer periods of time alone with his daughter. The longer he was alone with her, the more he came to realize that his fear of acting upon his impulses was unrealistic. During the first few practices Joel did not report progress. Instead he would have the thought, "I haven't killed because I haven't gone crazy yet. But what if I go crazy tomorrow?" With each additional practice, Joel learned that "Tomorrow has come and I'm still here, in control, with my daughter." With each passing day, he became increasingly convinced that it wasn't simply luck or chance that prevented him from killing his daughter.

Find *every opportunity you can* to face situations that cause you discomfort. What activities do you avoid in order to keep yourself or others safe? When do you hesitate to act, for fear that you will make a mistake? What events or places do you steer away from so that you won't begin to have distressing thoughts? These are the times when you need to be alert, for these times give you the opportunity to practice facing your fears. If you are a washer, go ahead and touch those doorknobs or wear those clothes after they have been "contaminated." If you are a checker, lock the doors of your home without having someone else check them. If you are a repeater, be willing to do things the "wrong" way. Orderers can let someone else straighten up the house, and hoarders can let someone else rearrange their "collections" or throw things out.

Often when you are in distressing situations your initial response will be to hesitate; you feel uncertain about whether you can handle the task. In such moments remind yourself of your long-term goals. You don't only seek to get rid of your obsessions; there are tasks you want to accomplish, pleasures you want to enjoy, relationships you want to pursue. Focus on these *positive* goals. Your obsessions stand in the way of a meaningful, fulfilling future. Don't just fight *against* your symptoms, fight *for* your life goals. Facing situations you have been avoiding is a step toward a new future.

Remember that when you first face distressing situations you will probably feel anxious. Use the skills we discussed in this chapter to reduce your tension. Take a Calming Breath or practice the Calming Counts (page 91), and remind yourself that anxiety decreases over time. Remember, you don't have to be alone in your struggle. Call a friend or a relative and tell him or her what you are trying to accomplish. Seek that person's understanding and support.

Once you have practiced facing one of your feared situations, don't just wait quietly for your worries to start again. Get busy! Focus your attention away from your obsessions by being active. Take a long walk, exercise, go to the movies, get involved with projects at work, or talk to a friend on the phone.

When you want to change your obsessional patterns, the single most important thing to remember is: Don't fight your obsession. If you are having difficulty making headway with these techniques, ask yourself, "Am I still *struggling* to get rid of my obsessions?" If you are, stop! You already know struggling doesn't work; that's what you've been doing prior to picking up this book. The success of the skills we've described here depends on your willingness to give up the struggle. When you stop the struggle you will begin to notice a significant difference. You actually *can* have control over your symptoms.

Some of you will notice immediate positive results from applying these skills. Others will progress steadily for several weeks, reducing their worries by half, then spend another two or three months working to gradually worry less and less. So don't get discouraged. If you are moderately or highly success-ful during the first weeks but find you're still obsessing some-what, continue practicing for several more weeks. You should notice improvement over time, even if it's not apparent every week.

If you practice daily for a few weeks and do not experience at least moderate relief, seek help from a mental-health profes-sional who is familiar with OCD treatment. This specialist can assist you in solving problems you might be having with apply-ing the self-help program and may be able to adapt these techniques so that they work better for you.

6 🐝

MASTERING YOUR COMPULSIONS

IN CHAPTER 1 we described how rituals persist because they provide temporary relief from obsessional distress. For some people, obsessions cause continuous distress, and only through ritualizing can they find peaceful moments. Therefore, rituals become very powerful. With time, compulsions often become increasingly rigid, so that those islands of peace are purchased at an extremely high price: The rituals take more and more of your time and eventually dominate your life.

Ultimately, getting rid of your OC symptoms means giving up the rituals. For now we propose that you temporarily delay the goal of ridding yourself completely of the compulsions so that you can focus your efforts on specific, smaller modifications. To prepare yourself for successful resistance, start by setting up more limited short-term goals. In this section we will describe four techniques you can use to start to prepare yourself to give up the rituals. The fifth self-help technique we will present will help you stop ritualizing altogether.

The first four self-help practices which will curtail your compulsions can be applied while you work on letting go of

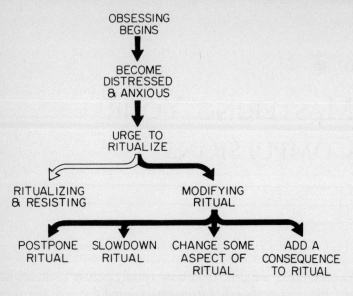

SELF-HELP OPTIONS FOR RITUALS

your obsessions. Alternatively, you can first work on your obsessions and then start changing your compulsions.

Read through the four practices and decide which ones you would like to try. There are no rules as to which you should try first or which will work better for certain rituals. However, when you choose one technique, give it enough opportunity to work for you. Don't simply dismiss a method because it isn't helpful the first few times.

SELF-HELP PRACTICE 1: POSTPONE RITUALIZING TO A SPECIFIC LATER TIME We have already discussed how to postpone your obsessions. Many of the same principles apply to compulsions here as well. If you have more than one ritual, select one you think might be the easiest to postpone. Then the next time you feel compelled to ritualize, delay it for a specified length of time. This is a mental ploy that will help you resist the ritual successfully because it requires resistance for only a short period of time. How long you postpone the ritualizing is a judgment you make based on what you think you can accomplish. Sometimes waiting thirty seconds is all you can tolerate. Other times, postponing for half a day is possible.

This practice will help in two ways. First, you will begin to tolerate longer periods of distress instead of instantly reducing the discomfort through ritualizing. Second, successful postponement will enhance your sense of control.

Like anxiety and distress, urges to ritualize decrease on their own over time, as long as you don't act on those urges. If you succeed in postponing the compulsive actions for several hours, you might discover that you no longer feel so compelled to engage in them when your time to ritualize arrives. Through this experience, you begin to believe that there may be other ways besides ritualizing to reduce your distress. Letting time pass and becoming distracted by other thoughts and feelings may successfully decrease the urge to ritualize.

As time goes by and your urge to ritualize diminishes, you will gain a sense of perspective, and with that perspective comes a greater sense of self-control. If you postponed ritualizing from 8:00 A.M. to 10:00 A.M., and you still experience the urge, you can postpone it again by saying to yourself, "I'll wait until noon and see how I'm doing then." If you can continue postponing, your urge will eventually fade away. If you cannot postpone again, apply one of the following two practices.

SELF-HELP PRACTICE 2: THINK AND ACT IN SLOW MOTION DURING THE RITUAL Another way to change your ritualistic pattern is to purposely slow down the thinking and physical movements that occur during the ritual itself. There are two major benefits to this practice. First, when you are distressed you often feel tense, pressured, and rushed. By slowing down your thoughts and actions, you decrease the intensity that accompanies the ritualizing. Without that intensity, the ritual may not be as compelling and consequently will lose some of its power.

The second significant component of slowing down during a ritual is that you will remember more of the details of your action. OC's often doubt that they have ritualized sufficiently. They feel safe momentarily but seconds later start doubting whether they carried out the rituals adequately. This leads them into another round of rituals. As you physically and mentally slow down, you can better remember the details of your actions. Since this technique provides you with a stronger memory of your actions, it will reduce your doubts.

This pattern of doubting and rechecking is exemplified by Scott, who had difficulty remembering where he had placed things and therefore continually had to check if items were in their proper location. An example was placing money in his wallet. Scott would open his wallet and place a bill into the fold. But he couldn't let it go. He had to repeatedly press it into the fold, and lift it out again, to make sure that the task was accomplished. When he finally was satisfied that the bill was indeed in the fold, he would attempt to close his wallet but couldn't. He had to reopen the wallet immediately and check the placement of the bill again, thinking, "Is it really there?" Placing money into his wallet could easily become a one-hour ordeal. This action was only one of many in which Scott could become stuck. To avoid getting stuck for hours in any given action, Scott would perform each movement very quickly.

Here is how Scott used this slow-motion practice successfully to overcome his wallet ritual. Several times a day he practiced inserting money into his wallet in the following manner. First, he opened the fold of the wallet slowly and gazed into it in a casual, rather than anxious, way. Simultaneously he took a nice long Calming Breath and relaxed his body. Fifteen seconds later he slowly inserted the bill into the fold and held it there with his fingers while continuing to gaze at it and to breathe in a relaxed manner. Next, in slow motion, he let go of the bill, gradually closed the fold, and then the wallet. This slow-motion process eventually allowed him to return to the normal mechanics of handling money comfortably.

Slow-motion practice can be used with many behavioral rituals. It is especially effective with checking rituals since it seems to reduce the checker's doubts about his actions. For instance, if you wish to practice slow-motion checking of a door, approach the door slowly, taking a few moments to take a Calming Breath and to casually study the lock. As your hand reaches the lock, notice the sensation of the metal on your fingers. If it is a dead bolt lock, then turn it ever so slowly. Listen for the click as the bolt drops into place. As soon as you hear it, pause for a moment. Hold your hand in place for fifteen more seconds while asking yourself, "Is this door locked?" When you respond, "Yes," drop your arm and slowly walk away.

When you practice this slow-motion procedure, be sure to incorporate either the Calming Breath or Calming Counts, discussed in Chapter 5. By interspersing them several times throughout, you can help keep your physical tension at a minimum. This, in turn, will help your concentration and your memory.

SELF-HELP PRACTICE 3: CHANGE SOME ASPECT OF YOUR RITUAL When choosing this practice you decide to change any of a variety of characteristics within your compulsive pattern. To do so you first need to analyze the specific manner in which you ritualize. Choose one ritual and analyze its characteristics according to the list that follows. Take a pencil and paper and jot down all the specific details you can think of. Describe your exact motions and thoughts, in the order they occur. When do you ritualize? How? Where?

CHARACTERISTICS OF RITUALS

- Specific actions
- Specific thoughts
- The order of the action
- The number of repetitions
- The particular objects used
- Physical stances
- Corresponding emotions
- Locations
- Special triggering thoughts or events

Begin altering some elements of your rituals, and practice those changes regularly over the next few days. This process will be the beginning of bringing this seemingly involuntary behavior under your voluntary control—not by totally stopping the ritual but by consciously manipulating it. Here are some examples:

Change the order in which you ritualize. For instance, if when you shower you start by washing your feet and methodically working your way up to your head, reverse your order by beginning with your head.

Change the frequency. If counting is part of your ritual, alter the numbers and the repetitions you require to complete the ritual. If you always do ten sets of four counts, do twelve sets of three counts. If you must put three and only three packs of sugar into your coffee cup, then put two half packs in and throw the rest away.

Change the objects you use. If you wash with a particular soap, change brands. If you tap your finger in repetitions on your calculator, tap the table just next to the calculator instead.

Change when you ritualize. If you have to dress and undress repeatedly, do each set in a different room. Change your posture during the ritual. If you always stand while ritualizing, then sit. If you always have your eyes open, then try your compulsion with your eyes closed.

There are three benefits to this practice. First, as is true for the other two practices in this section, you will be able to alter your compulsions without the great difficulty involved in trying to stop them altogether. Second, by changing important aspects of the ritualistic pattern, you are likely to break the powerful magic of the rituals. You will find out that the ritual brings temporary relief even when not performed perfectly. Hence, you introduce flexibility into the pattern. This disruption in the ritual is the beginning of its destruction. Third, this practice enhances your conscious awareness of when and how you perform your rituals. When you are ready to completely give up ritualizing, this awareness will enable you to recognize the first signs of your urge to ritualize and to stop yourself just before you automatically begin to do so.

Ruth was a twenty-four-year-old housewife who repeated actions in order to circumvent bad luck. Her rituals were pervasive, involving almost all daily activity. For example, when cleaning countertops or washing dishes, Ruth became stuck squeezing the sponge in several sets of ten. In her practice of changing the ritual, she continued squeezing the sponge, but now with each squeeze she passed the sponge from one hand to the other. This change caused considerable distress for Ruth, since she feared that the new routine would fail to protect herself and her loved ones. Nevertheless, she was determined to implement the change. After two weeks, instead of squeezing the sponge, Ruth started a new routine on her own. Now she simply tossed the sponge in the air from one hand to the other ten times. Soon thereafter she was able to resist the urge to squeeze altogether and could clean the counter in a normal manner.

Ruth also had a compulsion to rinse her hands while mentally counting to ten as she rubbed her hands together under the faucet. She tried a different approach with this problem. Upon having the urge to rinse her hands, Ruth held one hand under a light flow of cold water at the sink while gradually turning on the hot faucet with her other hand. At the same time, instead of counting, she subvocalized, "Cold . . . warm . . . warmer . . . hot!" Those words corresponded to the rising temperature. Just before the temperature became too hot to tolerate, Ruth removed her hand. A few minutes later she rinsed her other hand in the same manner.

You can see that this practice requires that you create new habits. These new actions are incompatible with your tendency to keep your original rituals unchanged. It is impossible to keep rigid rituals and at the same time continue to change them. This is why it is important to implement this practice. Changing your rituals is a big step toward giving them up entirely.

SELF-HELP PRACTICE 4: ADD A CONSEQUENCE TO YOUR RITUAL One simple change that can greatly increase your awareness is to add a consequence every time you ritualize. With this practice you need not change how or when you ritualize, but each time you *do* ritualize, you must then perform some additional task. Choose a task totally unrelated to any of your compulsive tendencies and also something that requires you to disrupt your normal routine. Decide to drive to a park and pick up trash for an hour, do some kind gesture for someone you are angry with, practice the piano for forty-five minutes, or hand-copy ten poems from a book. Ideally, the consequence you choose will also be one that has some redeeming value. A consequence often chosen by OC's is exercise—such as taking a brisk walk for thirty minutes.

If these sound like disruptive, time-consuming tasks it's because they are supposed to be! Yet do not perceive them as punishment. To be effective, the consequences must be costly. Because they are costly in time and effort, after some practice you will become aware of the moment you are about to ritualize, and you will hesitate. You will pause to think about whether it is best to start ritualizing. This moment of hesitation gives you an opportunity to resist the compulsion in order to avoid that costly consequence.

Let's say you must ritualistically check the stove every time you leave the house for work in the morning. You tend to get stuck touching each knob six times before you walk out the door. Later, when you are on the front porch, you doubt whether the stove is off and back you go for another round of checking. Several weeks ago you began to use the slow-motion practice every time you checked. This has worked so well that now you check the stove only once and never touch the knobs. But each day, standing out on the front porch, you still become doubtful and must return to the stove for a second quick check "just to be sure."

This would be a good time to implement a consequence. Decide that, starting tomorrow, each time you check the stove again, touch a knob while checking, or even glance at the knobs again while walking through the kitchen, you must take a brisk thirty-minute walk as soon as you come home from work. This means you take a walk before doing *anything* else: no stopping at the store on the way home; no having a snack after you get home. Just put on your walking shoes and go, regardless of whether it's hot and muggy, raining, or snowing. Soon you will be thinking twice before stepping back inside from the porch "just to make sure."

This technique will work in the same way whether you are a washer who wants to stop washing your hands a second time, a hoarder who wants to stop collecting meaningless materials, or an orderer who wants to stop straightening up repeatedly. If the consequence you choose does not have this intended effect after numerous trials, then switch to a consequence that seems a little more costly.

SELF-HELP PRACTICE 5: CHOOSE NOT TO RITUALIZE This, of course, is the option you will continually take as you gain full control of your rituals. Yet it requires determination. You must have a long-term commitment to overcome your problem in order to counterbalance the immediate urge to ritualize. You must be willing to suffer short-term distress in order to achieve your goal of freeing yourself from your symptoms.

All of the previous techniques in this section promote your ability to refrain from ritualizing and help prepare you for this option. Each aids in developing the important position of choice. Working with any of the other options first—postponing, going in slow motion, changing some aspect of the ritual, or adding a consequence—helps you choose this last option with less anxiety, stress, and effort than if you used it first. Instead of saying, "I *have* to stop this," you are much more likely to feel, "I'm ready to stop this."

To decide not to ritualize is to decide to *face your anxiety directly,* to *stop protecting yourself from your distressful feelings* through your compulsive behavior. You are willing to feel anxious if that's necessary. In fact, that is a lesson you will learn through your practice of this option. You will discover you can manage your discomfort. To find this out, you will go toward your anxiety instead of away from it.

The best way to do this is to voluntarily initiate contact with whatever it is that brings on your urge and then withhold your rituals. If you have an irrational fear of contamination, touch things you believe are contaminated. If you are afraid you might leave the stove on accidentally, then purposely turn it on and leave the house for half an hour. If you have to have a perfectly clean house, then mess up several rooms and leave them that way for several days at a time. Only through this practice can you discover that your distress passes and so does your urge. Chapters 7 and 8 provide specific instructions on how to stop your rituals.

But you don't simply have to grit your teeth and bear your distress. Refer back to pages 90 and 91, where we described the breathing techniques. Use the Calming Breath and the Calming Counts to help let go of your tension. Be sure to refocus your attention on some other task that will hold your interest, like talking to a supportive friend or taking a brisk walk.

How will you feel after several weeks of withholding your rituals? Here is how one checker experienced the change. Vann had been struggling with his symptoms for eighteen months before he began to apply these self-help skills. During his worst periods, he would become involved in checking rituals up to five hours a day. Table 7, which follows, lists most of the items he checked on a daily basis. Checking involved a minimum of six or seven attempts at verifying that each item was OK. Often his concern was that he had missed seeing something he should have noticed: new scratches or dents on the trash can, dust particles under the telephone, an inappropriate item in the basement. Other times he checked as a way to prevent a disaster: An electrical cord will be wrapped around the trash can; his son will trip over some item on his bedroom floor; a fire will start in the kitchen or a flood will occur in the basement. Some days Vann would check a particular item over a hundred times.

TABLE 7:
VANN'S DAILY CHECKING RITUALS

At Home in the Morning
Bathrooms
Closets
Lights
Sinks

Bathroom doors
Top drawers of dressers

At Work
Trash can
Files
Drawers
Phone book
Bottom of phone
Placement of phone
Placement of files
Placement of trash can
Spots on floor
Spots on baseboard
Key to desk
Phone—on and off
Bathroom faucets and toilet
Lights—on and off
Coffeepot
Office-door lock
Building-door lock

Car
Doors shut
Armrest—raise and lower
Ashtray
Steering wheel
Radio
Air conditioner and heater
Trash on floor
Under dashboard
Under seats

At Home in the Evening
Outside faucets
Gas grill
Garage windows and doors
Rabbit pen and gate
Garbage can and top
Entrance gates

Back door
Mailbox
Clean eyeglasses repeatedly
Briefcase
Calculator

At Bedtime
Doors and locks
Thermostat
Bathrooms: faucets, toilet and lid, shower curtain, medicine
  cabinet, window, night light, toothpaste caps, toothbrushes
TV
Lights
Refrigerator
Basement light and door
All kitchen appliances
Radio
Fireplace
Son's bedroom: plugs, phone cord, articles off floor, son OK in
  bed, drawers

We interviewed Vann ten weeks into his self-help program, when he was still practicing confronting his fears on a daily basis. By this time he had made significant improvement on about 75 percent of his rituals. Here are some excerpts from that conversation, during which he describes his progress in a few areas:

Locking the house at night is really no problem now. I used to go to bed at eight o'clock because I didn't want to have to perform locking rituals. I was afraid I was going to get stuck checking. If I came in at nine-thirty and my wife had already gone to bed, then I was stuck until twelve o'clock locking the house. So I always tried to go to bed before she did so she could do all of the locking of the house.

Now I am staying up until eleven or eleven-thirty, reading books, doing things I have always wanted to do but couldn't in the last year and a half. I generally just check the doors one time; I never go back to check them again. Some nights when I walk through the kitchen I check the toaster oven to make sure it's off. I don't check it five or six times, I just look at it one time, touch the control to make sure it's turned off, and then walk out of the kitchen. Other nights I may not check it at all. In the past when I checked it I was afraid it was going to be left on and the house would catch on fire. That thought really doesn't come into my head anymore.

Only through his personal experience did Vann learn this necessary lesson: He doesn't have to ritualize to get rid of his anxiety.

If I can control the first ten seconds of checking, and if I can stop it early, I'm fine. Two months ago when I practiced, I still had a desire two hours later to check that item. That desire is much less now.

I can remember in the past being stuck for two hours one afternoon in the office looking at that phone book, taking it in and out of the drawer thirty, forty, fifty times. Before I put it back in the drawer I had to keep looking at all the things about the phone book: checking the scratches on it, making sure all the pages weren't crumpled up, and so forth. What I do now is pick the phone book up, close it, shove it into the drawer, and shut the drawer. I haven't had too much of a problem doing that either. It really gave me a lot of confidence to accomplish that.

Vann's primary technique now is to confront his fear of becoming stuck checking if he checks just once. Notice how he finds every opportunity he can to practice his skills. He is convinced, through his recent successes, that his best approach is frequent encounters with his fears.

In the past I would pull out the backseat of the car, and if there was dirt there, I would have to clean it up. If a bolt was there I would look at it and get stuck on the backseat, focused on that bolt.

Now I do all of this intentionally. I lift up the backseat and try to make something really bother me, try to feel anxious. I would feel that anxiety, replace the backseat, shut the back door of the car, and walk away. Again, that has helped tremendously because I don't feel anxious about the car anymore.

When I first started walking away I felt really anxious. I wanted to go back and look at something under that seat again. I felt as though I didn't look at it hard enough, and I'd want to look at it again. I would sweat a little bit, my heart would beat faster, I'd become very irritable, and I felt very compulsive. I wanted to go check again! But I just decided I wasn't going to do it. Sure enough, about two hours later the desire went away.

In the beginning the desire would last awhile. However, if I checked the car today, I would have a very difficult time finding something that would catch my eye and make me anxious. The desire may last a minute or two and then go away.

I am really able to do things now I couldn't do before, like playing tennis, or relaxing with my children in the evening. I feel really great. It has been a little difficult over the last six weeks, but it's so much easier than it was in the first four weeks. I try to just take one thing at a time and not try to do too much. The key thing is to get your confidence up. From the beginning I have really been trying to keep a lot of willpower, to just do it and face the consequences. I think it made a difference to have done it this way.

PART III

The Intensive Three-Week Program

7 ❦

TREATMENT FOR RITUALIZERS

THE INTENSIVE THREE-WEEK Program is the more intensive of the two programs presented in this book. It is based on an approach used by mental-health specialists who treat OCD. As we mentioned in Chapter 1, this approach is called "cognitive-behavioral therapy." It has been extensively researched in many centers around the world and is now considered the psychotherapy of choice for this disorder.

As we have suggested earlier you should first practice the skills of the Initial Self-Help Program presented in Part II. This is the only program you need if you suffer from worries and obsessions. If you also suffer from compulsions, practice the skills described in Chapter 5. However, if you are spending more than two hours a day ritualizing or if you have not gained sufficient control over your thoughts or actions even after following the Initial Self-Help Program, then you should move on to Part III.

In this chapter we will help you understand the basic principles of the treatment program which relies a great deal on self-help. Patients don't simply *talk* about their problems with the therapist; rather, they learn skills that help them gain control over their symptoms. In the first part of this chapter we will present the program in detail. Starting on page 131, we will describe special treatments for the individual types of OCD. After reading the opening section you may want to turn to the treatment programs which apply to your specific concerns and use them as models for generating your own self-help program described in Chapter 8.

In Chapter 8 we will take you through the planning of your own self-help program. Separate plans are provided for washers, checkers, repeaters, hoarders, orderers, and thinking ritualizers. If you decide to follow these intensive self-help programs, we encourage you to do so with the help of a supportive friend, family member, or mental-health professional. Chapter 9 discusses medications that might help you to confront your symptoms, and in Chapter 10 you will learn just how successfully you can rid yourself of these symptoms and return to a normal life. Five recovered obsessive-compulsives share their struggles and accomplishments with you. Like them, you too can get better, no matter how long you have had your symptoms or how trapped you feel now.

It is only recently that we have really started to help people who suffer from obsessions and/or compulsions. Individuals who sought treatment for OCD in the past had at best limited success in getting rid of their symptoms. Traditional psychotherapies—psychoanalysis, dynamic psychotherapy, and supportive therapy—were often helpful in one aspect or another, but on the whole did not decrease obsessions or compulsions.

Effective treatment did not exist before the mid-1960s. In 1966 Dr. Victor Meyer, at the Middlesex Hospital in England, developed a radical but simple program for treatment of obsessive-compulsive washers, which he later applied to other types of ritualizers. The program began by identifying situations that "contaminated" the patients and promoted their urge to ritualize. After composing this list, Dr. Meyer progressively confronted the patients with each situation.

However, simply exposing an OC to a contaminant is not enough. Washers routinely touch contaminated things but then wash off the contamination and thereby restore a state of cleanliness. So Dr. Meyer introduced a second procedure into the program. He prevented the patients from engaging in ritualistic washing and cleaning so that they stayed contaminated for long periods.

This program was so successful that clinical centers around the world began to use this approach, research it, and modify it. After five years of experimenting, the Center for the Treatment and Study of Anxiety at the Medical College of Pennsylvania, in Philadelphia, devised a successful three-week treatment program for OCD. It now includes three components, which we will call *exposure, imagery practice,* and *ritual prevention.*

During *exposure,* the patients are confronted with the situations that provoke their discomfort. After several treatment sessions, their anxiety decreases. The obsessions of washers lend themselves readily to this kind of treatment. If you feel contaminated by contact with the floor, you must sit on the floor for extended lengths of time. If you feel contaminated by your hometown, you must visit it for prolonged periods of time. Soon those situations will no longer make you as anxious as they once did.

For many OC's the obsessions occur within their imagination and rarely take place in reality. This makes it impossible for them to practice remaining in those situations for prolonged periods. For example, if a person fears that her home will burn down, we certainly do not wish to have her house catch on fire in order to subject her to her fear in reality. Similarly, someone who fears that he has run over a person who is now lying in the road cannot be exposed in reality to such a situation.

If confrontation with the feared situation is necessary to reduce obsessions, how can patients improve without directly confronting their fears? They can confront these scenes through imagery, which helps them visualize the feared circumstances. In *imagery practice,* the patients create detailed mental pictures of the terrible consequences they fear will occur if they do not engage in their ritualistic behavior. During prolonged exposure to these images, their distress level gradually decreases.

When OC's encounter their feared situations or their obsessional thoughts, they become anxious and feel compelled to perform the ritualistic behavior as a way to reduce their distress. Exposure techniques cause this same distress and urge to ritualize. But in treatment, *ritual prevention* is added. This requires that patients completely eliminate ritualistic behaviors. By facing their fears without resorting to their compulsions, OC's gradually become less anxious. Behavior therapists call this process *habituation.*

TABLE 8:
THE COMPONENTS OF TREATMENT FOR RITUALIZERS

Exposure: Staying for long periods in the presence of a feared object or situation that evokes anxiety and distress, e.g., actual contact with contaminants.

Imagery Practice: Mentally visualizing oneself in the feared situations or visualizing their consequences, e.g., driving on the road and hitting a pedestrian.

Ritual Prevention: Refraining from ritualistic behavior, e.g., leaving the kitchen without checking the stove, or touching the floor without washing one's hands.

Habituation: Reduction of fear during prolonged or repeated exposure to a feared object or situation.

How Three Negative Beliefs Change

Why do exposure, imagery practice, and ritual prevention work? Consider again how rituals persist. A person gets distressed by certain situations or certain mental images. He or she performs a specific ritualistic behavior that provides short-term relief. In the long run, however, this ritualizing only serves to continually reaffirm three negative beliefs: (1) I have to avoid the distressing situation, or else my intense distress will continue forever; (2) the rituals will keep me or others safe; and (3) I must ritualize to keep myself from going crazy.

Let's consider this first belief. People suffering from this disorder believe that they have to avoid the distressing situation, or else their intense distress will continue forever. This belief causes them to avoid many situations or to ritualize if they cannot avoid them. Most of us already know that anxiety does not continue forever. If we can help OC's remain in the distressful situation, they too will realize their beliefs were mistaken.

During prolonged exposure, intense anxiety gradually decreases. This is what we mean by habituation. If you place someone in an anxiety-provoking situation for an hour or two and ask him to rate every ten minutes just how anxious he is, you will find that he gradually becomes less anxious, until the anxiety is no longer present. If you measure his heart rate during this same period, you will find similar results. Initially his heart will beat faster, but it gradually slows down until it reaches its original level prior to confronting the fear. As his anxiety drops through habituation, he is better able to think rationally. In the future, when these same situations occur spontaneously, he will react with some anxiety, some distress, but not with terror.

You will be able to use this same process of exposure to overcome your fears. It can be successful whether you are afraid of entering public bathrooms, driving alone, inviting guests into your home, or handling a knife. When you first begin to face these situations you will feel anxious. However, if you return to these same situations again and again for longer periods of time, your distress will gradually diminish. Eventually your belief that your anxiety will last forever is challenged. You now know that you can think "If I just wait it out, my anxiety will diminish."

The second common belief is "In order to keep myself or others safe, I must ritualize." Most people think of their own death, or that of a loved one, with sorrow and regret but without undue anxiety. But obsessive-compulsives who worry about dying or causing death become devastated. In the same way, OC's who worry about their house burning down, or God punishing them, or leaving behind an injured person, react to such thoughts with extreme distress. This intense reaction prevents them from evaluating rationally how dangerous the situation is and how much actual protection they receive by ritualizing. The hand washer thinks "Yes, I did contaminate myself with those germs and it's true that I haven't become sick or spread disease to my family. But that is because I washed my hands very carefully." The checker thinks "It's true my house didn't burn down, but that's because I was extremely careful and checked repeatedly to make sure all appliances were unplugged." This kind of logic justifies continuing the rituals.

Yet this too is challenged when you confront feared situations. For instance, Richard, who feared that people would laugh at him if they saw him write "I'm a fraud," learned through his exposure practice that it was not a disaster to write those words on a hundred checks. Nobody laughed at him. By exposing OCD sufferers to situations they fear might cause distress, and by preventing them from enacting their rituals, this program enables them to come to important realizations. The patient can now say, "I have faced threatening situations without protecting myself and still nothing bad happened."

For exposure practice to be effective, it is important that patients become emotionally in touch with their fears. The more they experience their distress during the exposure sessions, the more they are able to overcome those fears. So during exposure it is important to contemplate the disastrous consequences that might occur as a result of such exposure. For example, if we direct a patient to a public toilet and ask him to touch that toilet, we want him to simultaneously think that he may get VD as a result of that touching. Later on, when the patient realizes he did not get VD, he learns his fear was unjustified. This reduces his distress. In the same way, during imagery practice, patients are asked to become emotionally involved with detailed images of pending disasters and to imagine them as vividly as they can.

A third common belief is "I must ritualize. If I don't [wash, repeat, check] I'll go crazy." This belief by itself encourages OC's to ritualize when they find themselves distressed again. This belief, too, is challenged through exposure. Geraldine, who felt contaminated by her mother, discovered that when she stayed in contact for a long time with her mother's clothes, she could become relatively calm without having to wash. During her program, Geraldine did not wash her hands and felt extremely anxious for a week and she discovered that she did not go crazy. In fact, as time passed she became less and less anxious.

Similarly, as you practice exposure, imagery practice, and ritual prevention in your self-help program, you will gradually learn how irrational your obsessions are, how unnecessary it is to avoid distress at all cost, and how unlikely it is that your worst scenarios will come true. It's true that when you are highly distressed you *feel* as though it will never end and you think that you *must* ritualize to feel safe or to keep from being overwhelmed. Yet by following these guidelines and with the support of people close to you, you will find the courage to challenge these beliefs. The first few times will always be the hardest, but once you start noticing changes, you will develop the confidence required to conquer your symptoms.

The Program Design

The program we use at the Center for the Treatment and Study of Anxiety at the Medical College of Pennsylvania includes fifteen exposure practices of two hours each over three weeks, plus two to four hours of daily homework. Treatment usually begins by using imagery practice, which involves asking the patient to imagine the disastrous consequences he fears. The therapist describes the situation while the patient visualizes it.

There are two reasons why we want to begin therapy with imagery practice. First, it is often easier for patients to face their fears in reality if they have already been exposed to the feared situation in imagery. *Imagining* yourself being contaminated by touching a toilet seat is less frightening than actually doing so in reality. At the same time, it prepares you for the time when you will touch one. Second, only through imagery can we confront patients with their most feared disasters, such as causing their home to burn down.

After about forty-five minutes of imagery practice, the patient is confronted with a real situation or object that will trigger his or her obsession. This obsession will usually lead to the urge to ritualize. Yet he or she is not allowed to engage in any ritualistic behaviors for the entire three weeks.

Exposure is done gradually over the three-week period, beginning with situations that produce a moderate level of anxiety. If patients start with a behavior that produces very low distress, they will not learn to be courageous and confront their fears. On the other hand, starting with situations that cause overwhelming distress will make it difficult to realize mistaken thinking.

So exposure begins with situations that produce moderate discomfort. Every day a new, more difficult situation is added. After a week the patient is usually ready to confront the most disturbing situation. During the next two weeks, new situations are incorporated into the treatment.

Because of its successful outcome, this treatment is considered by many OCD experts to be the most effective treatment for this disorder. Let's look at how it is applied to the different kinds of OC rituals.

The Treatment of Washers

Washers, as we have discussed earlier, feel contaminated by certain situations or objects. Contamination is highly distressing and this distress is temporarily offset by washing and cleaning rituals. Some washers feel that contamination will lead to illness or death—their own or that of others. Other washers fear they will suffer nervous breakdowns as a result of the continued distress caused by contamination.

We will illustrate the treatment of washers by describing the treatment program of three patients. We have selected these cases to represent three somewhat different treatment approaches. By now you have analyzed your own problem. If you are a washer, you can decide which of the three cases is most similar to yours and use it as a model for devising your own self-help program, described in Chapter 8.

PHIL Phil was a typical washer who felt contaminated by bodily secretions and was afraid that such contact would make him sick. His treatment included exposure to bodily secretions, imagery practice with the consequences he feared, and ritual prevention—that is, blocking his washing and cleaning rituals.

As a consequence of his fear of bodily secretions, Phil also avoided contact with people or objects touched by other people. In his mind most people were not thorough enough in washing their hands after using the toilet. Therefore, everything they touched was contaminated. Places touched by a large number of people were especially contaminated. The most distressing situations for Phil are listed as follows, with numbers indicating how distressing they were on a scale of 0 to 100:

Touching a doorknob: 55
Touching a newspaper: 65
Touching someone's sweaty shirt: 75
Touching toilet seats in public bathrooms: 85
Touching spots of urine or feces on toilet paper: 100

On the first day of treatment, Phil and his therapist went downtown to a large building where there were lots of people walking in and out. For Phil, touching doorknobs in such a building produced 55 on his distress scale, so exposure started there. He repeatedly touched the doorknobs of the main doors with his right hand and every few minutes noticed how distressed he was, using his distress scale. Phil ended this practice after twenty-five minutes, when his distress level was down to 20. He then held the doorknob with his left hand. His distress level increased to 30. Next, Phil rubbed his contaminated hands on his face and ran them through his hair and over his clothes. The level of his distress and sense of contamination rose to 40. (This rise is natural when contamination is transferred from the hands to other parts of the body.)

At the end of the session, Phil rubbed a napkin on one of the doorknobs and put the contaminated napkin in his pocket. On returning home that day, he contaminated his entire apartment with that napkin. He rubbed the napkin all over the clothes in his closet, over his dishes, on the kitchen counter, on everything in his underwear drawers, and on his bed sheets and pajamas. Phil kept up this activity until he felt that every possible place in the house was contaminated. In this way, home was no longer a place of safety where he could avoid outside contamination.

The next day, Phil and his therapist went to another public building and practiced in the same way. By the end of this session, Phil felt free of distress, and the doorknob had lost its power to contaminate him. On the same day Phil started confronting his fear of newspapers in the way described for the doorknob.

On day three, Phil began to confront his concerns about sweat. With the therapist's support, he placed one of his hands in his bare armpit, and the other inside one of his shoes. Doing this, he felt a distress level of 70. Phil maintained that contact until his shoe and armpit distress was down to 30. He then took out his sweaty hands and rubbed them on his face, his head, his clothes. At home, he contaminated the house in the same manner described for the doorknob.

By the fourth day, Phil felt very little discomfort or contamination during contact with newspapers, doorknobs, and sweat. Therapy then focused on contact with toilets. Starting with the bathroom in the therapist's office, Phil placed his hands on the toilet seat and kept them there until his sense of contamination reduced from 80 to 40. He then rubbed his contaminated hands on his face, hair, and clothes. He rubbed a piece of toilet paper on the toilet seat, to be used later for spreading contamination all over his apartment.

By the fifth day, sweat and toilet seats aroused little discomfort, and newspapers and doorknobs no longer bothered him. He could then focus his attention on confronting his fear of urine.

By day six, Phil was comfortable with the toilet seat and

with sweat, but urine was still a problem. So the therapist postponed introducing feces until day seven, and decided to add another hour of exposure to his fear of urine. Phil was asked to bring to the session a container full of his own urine. He moistened a paper towel with the urine and rubbed it on his hands, hair, and clothes. Phil practiced this for three hours that day.

On day seven, Phil began his exposure to feces. He slightly soiled a piece of toilet paper with his own fecal material, using an amount so minimal it was not enough to spread feces on his skin but enough for him to feel that the toilet paper was highly contaminated. It led to an 80 on the distress scale. Phil rubbed the toilet paper on his hands, face, and clothes and later contaminated objects throughout his home with it. For the next two weeks, Phil continued to practice by approaching public toilets and crowded places, touching strangers on the street, and carrying used toilet paper in his pocket.

During the same days that Phil was practicing his exposure, his therapist asked him to write a story about what would happen if he went to a public bathroom and allowed a few drops of urine to touch his body or clothes. Phil wrote a detailed story describing the harm he feared would follow. In his story, several hours after exposure to those drops of urine, he begins to feel sick; the germs from the public toilet have caught up with him. He develops diarrhea, vomiting, nausea, and a high temperature, and lies in bed sweating because he has caught some unknown toilet germs. The therapist then asked him to imagine this detailed scene as vividly as possible and describe it aloud into a forty-five-minute audiotape.

Twice a day for the entire first week Phil listened to this tape. During the first two sessions his mind wandered; he had great difficulty concentrating on the images, which he wanted to avoid. The therapist supported his attempts and continued to explain to Phil the importance of being in touch with his uncomfortable feelings throughout the time he listened to the tape. By the third session Phil could pay attention to the entire tape. Usually about ten minutes of listening was required to become emotionally involved with the scenes. The images produced extreme distress initially. Phil's face twitched, his body became tense, and he felt intense anxiety. However, during each subsequent session, Phil became a little less anxious. Once he no longer felt distress while listening to the tape, Phil was asked to write another story to be recorded.

In the second story Phil is touching his own feces and again develops diarrhea symptoms, only this time the illness is much more severe, and he feels much worse. He is admitted into the hospital because he is dehydrated. The doctors are not sure whether he will live.

Phil listened to this imagery tape twice a day during the second week. By the end of that week he felt he could confront these images and thoughts without feeling immensely distressed. During this same time, of course, he continued to confront his contaminations through exposure.

Since the beginning of the treatment program, Phil was also following ritual-prevention instructions. In the first week he was allowed two ten-minute showers with very little soap and without any repetitive ritualizing; hand washing was not allowed at all. In the second week Phil was instructed to take a daily ten-minute unritualized shower. He was asked to wash his hands only twice daily, for thirty seconds each time, but never after he used the toilet. Immediately after washing his hands, Phil contaminated himself with the contaminant he was confronting on that particular day.

During the third week Phil was allowed five hand washings a day (but still never after using the toilet) and one ten-minute shower a day. He was instructed to keep up this regimen for three months following treatment. Phil was also asked to take every opportunity over those three months to use public toilets. In this way he developed a consistent habit of confronting contamination instead of avoiding it.

Phil has been practically free of symptoms for four years. Once in a while, after he has used a very dirty public toilet, he feels an urge to wash more than once. Yet he resists the urge to wash again, and within two hours his distress dissipates.

GERALDINE Geraldine, who was described in Chapter 2, felt contaminated by her mother but did not feel that contact with her would lead to illness. Despite this absence of feared consequences, her treatment included imagery practice because she was extremely distressed by the idea of actual contact with contaminants.

During the first stage of treatment, the therapist gathered information about Geraldine's problem, asking questions similar to those outlined in Chapter 3. He asked her to identify the situations that made her feel most distressed. On the top of her list was "being touched by Mother," especially on her hair. (Geraldine was highly sensitive to being touched on her head.) Being touched by her mother was the worst situation she could envision with respect to her OC symptoms. Thus, she rated this situation 100 on her distress scale. Other disturbing situations were:

Touching the local newspaper: 40
Touching the mail: 50
Touching money with her bare hands without washing it first: 60
Touching her husband's work clothes: 70
Wearing her mother's clothes: 90

In the first session Geraldine was asked to imagine that she had walked down the street, stopped near a newspaper stand, and bought the local paper. She then was to imagine spreading the newspaper all over herself. The therapist encouraged her to see in her mind's eye the face of her mother's neighbor, who worked at the newspaper. She was to imagine this man shopping at the same supermarket as her mother, touching products her mother had touched, and walking the same floors. Geraldine focused on the idea that the man carried that contamination from the mother's neighborhood into the newspaper's offices, thereby transferring it to Geraldine now that she was touching the paper. Geraldine felt quite anxious during the forty-five minutes in which she repeated this imagery. Yet she was able to tolerate that distress and continue the practice.

The second task during the first treatment session is to help the patient make direct contact with the actual feared situation. The therapist had previously acquired a copy of Geraldine's local newspaper in preparation for this session. He asked her to touch the paper with one hand, then pick it up with her other hand. These two simple moves required several minutes and much support from the therapist, since they represented direct contamination. Next, Geraldine was asked to touch her face with the paper, then to touch her clothes with it. At the end of the first session, the therapist instructed Geraldine to take the paper home and contaminate her entire house with it, including the dishes and all of her clothes. She was asked to take a piece of the newspaper to bed with her and sleep with it through the night. Within twenty-four hours Geraldine felt completely comfortable touching the newspaper.

On day two, Geraldine began working with her fear of money. Following the same techniques he used with the newspaper, the therapist encouraged her to hold the money, touch the bills and coins all over her clothes, and take them home with her to contaminate various areas of the house.

On day three she worked directly with her husband's contaminated clothes. By the fourth day of treatment Geraldine allowed her husband, Bob, to return home from work without calling her first. He opened the gate and front door by himself. To his relief after so many years, he did not have to go down into the basement for his mandatory shower. Instead, he walked into the house and sat on each of the chairs and sofas. He dragged his overcoat through the entire house as a way to further contaminate the surroundings. That night Bob wore his work clothes to bed in order to contaminate it. By day five the therapist had received a box containing some of Geraldine's mother's clothes. That day, Geraldine wore her mother's clothes during the therapy session and at home.

Although we are briefly presenting the events of this first week, we do not want to imply that Geraldine easily accomplished her goals. She felt determined to overcome her problem but was also anxious and hesitant throughout the treatment program. Several times, as a result of discomfort, she burst into tears, but each day she persevered and completed her tasks.

On day six the therapist invited Geraldine's mother to the treatment session. This was their first face-to-face contact in six years. Both were happy that they could finally see each other, but at the same time Geraldine was extremely anxious. By the end of the session, Geraldine allowed her mother to hug her while sitting next to her on a sofa. Mother then spent the weekend at her daughter's house, using Geraldine's towels in the bathroom, walking throughout the house, and contaminating it with her presence. Geraldine handled the visit well.

For the next two weeks Geraldine visited relatives she had avoided for the past six years. She stayed in her mother's home several nights, shopped with her, and gradually became involved in activities with her mother that had been commonplace in the past.

By the end of the three-week treatment, Geraldine felt no distress around her mother. Her long nightmare had come to an end.

As her symptoms subsided, more realistic questions about the mother-daughter relationship became apparent. Geraldine recalled that prior to the beginning of her OCD problem she used to visit her mother daily. Now she preferred to limit the frequency of their visits. Mother and daughter continued in supportive psychotherapy for ten more sessions in order to discuss how to restructure their relationship. Today they continue to have a close relationship and visit with each other periodically.

SUSAN In some instances, imagery practice is omitted from the program. Such treatment is illustrated by the story of Susan, who felt contaminated by her hometown. Susan, whose case was discussed in Chapter 2, had previously been through a behavioral treatment program that included exposure and limited ritual prevention. She had, in fact, benefited from that program, which she underwent while she lived in England. However, a few years later she moved back to the United States to live about a hundred miles from her hometown. After this move Susan began to experience her OCD symptoms again. She was afraid to visit her hometown, see her mother or other relatives, or approach any object that might have been directly or indirectly contaminated by association with this town.

In reviewing her previous treatment, the therapist found that Susan had never confronted her most feared situations. Since she was living in England during her treatment program, she didn't have an opportunity to visit her parents still living in the hometown. Instead, the therapy had focused on exposure to objects from home that Susan already had in her possession and on situations that interfered with her daily living in England. Those situations included confronting several boxes of Susan's college books that she had placed in the attic. There were also several kitchen objects that she had brought with her from the United States that thus were contaminated. She stored them in a remote corner, to avoid contact with them.

Susan's treatment in England addressed these objects, and she learned to feel comfortable in their presence. Other objects from her hometown were not a current problem to her, since they were not present in England. However, on returning to the United States, she had to face her old fears again.

In preparation for her second treatment program, Susan was asked to rate her discomfort regarding a variety of situations. She was most afraid to enter the attic of her original home. She was also afraid to wear her mother's clothes and touch the family Christmas ornaments. The therapist obtained some of these items from her home: ornaments, clothes from her mother, some of her own clothes that were left at home, books, cereal produced by the town's cereal company, and a coat manufactured by the town's coat factory.

The first two days of treatment were devoted to confronting the objects included in her first treatment, such as the books and kitchen objects. On day three the therapist brought into the office a cereal box from her hometown's company. Susan became overwhelmed with fear and refused to touch the box. Gradually the therapist calmed her down and asked her to touch the box first with one finger, then another. By the middle of the session, she was eating some of the cereal and feeling relatively comfortable. She was sent home that day with two cereal boxes and instructed to contaminate her house with them and to eat some of the cereal once an hour during the day.

As the program progressed, Susan began wearing her mother's and sister's clothes and some of her own clothes from home. By the sixth day she was able to touch the Christmas ornaments. Interestingly, touching the ornaments made her feel not anxious but sad. Susan had been afraid of feeling this deep sadness because it brought up unhappy memories of her hometown, Christmas, and other childhood experiences.

During the second weekend of treatment, the therapist accompanied Susan to her hometown. They sat for hours in the attic while Susan continued to remember unhappy times as a child in this house. Over the next week, she visited her mother and bought a coat from the local factory.

It is now eight years since Susan was treated. Occasionally she will experience a few moments of sadness when looking at one of the objects she has from her hometown. Her sadness at present no longer has the intensity it once had. She visits her parents regularly and is working productively at a job she enjoys.

Susan's second treatment was more successful because she finally confronted her greatest fears, especially the distressing situations in her hometown.

You should bear this in mind when you devise your self-help program. Confronting only a few of your feared situations will not lead to lasting improvement. Learning to handle comfortably *all* feared situations is essential to your complete recovery.

The Treatment of Checkers and Repeaters

Generating treatment programs for checkers and repeaters requires somewhat more creativity and imagination than programs for washers do. This is because of three difficulties.

First, it is more difficult to identify the exact situations that create anxiety in checkers. For repeaters, often there are no external situations precipitating the urge to ritualize. Second, because of the nature of their worries, it is hard to create situations in which a checker or a repeater will remain distressed for a prolonged time period. Third, in contrast to washers who always feel an urge to wash when contaminated, checkers vary in their urge to ritualize in seemingly similar situations. For example, checkers who are afraid a burglar might break into their home will check and recheck doors and windows. Yet if they visit someone else's home, they will not have the urge to check because they don't feel personally responsible for someone else's house. Therefore, it is much more difficult to conduct treatment of checkers in a therapist's office or clinic, where the urge to check often does not arise. Checkers need much of their therapy to be conducted in their own home or office, and the logistics of arranging for a therapist to visit the patient at home or at work can slow down the treatment process.

As described earlier, checkers try to prevent disastrous consequences that may result from their being neglectful. The core of their concerns is the image of the disasters they can cause. Since such disasters cannot be enacted in reality, imagery practice is used more frequently with checkers than with washers. Treatment also focuses more on preventing the checking behavior (ritual prevention) than on exposure. With washers, equal time is spent on both.

DAVID To illustrate the treatment of a checker, consider David, whose symptoms are described in Chapter 2. David was afraid of killing any living creature, was terrified by the thought that he might drop his two-year-old daughter and cause her death, and was concerned that he might hit a pedestrian inadvertently while driving his car.

The therapist asked David to generate a hierarchy of his feared disasters. He was most afraid of causing his daughter's death, followed by causing the death of a pedestrian, and then by the thought of killing a bug.

David's treatment began by confronting his least distressing concern—his fear of killing bugs. In the first session he was asked to imagine the following scene: He is walking on a lawn. He decides not to watch his footsteps as he typically would. Suddenly he looks back and realizes he has just stepped on an anthill. He begins to feel terribly guilty because he knows he could have avoided this destruction. He was also asked to imagine flushing the toilet and a moment later noticing that a live moth was whirling around in the water and finally flushed down the pipes.

Each of the scenes were fifteen to twenty minutes long and were repeated three times per session. David was asked to dwell on every distressing detail in each image: how awful he feels as he sees some of the ants squirm and then die, how guilty he becomes as he watches the moth trying in vain to flap its wings in the water, how careless he has been with God's creatures, acting as though he is more important than other living things.

After three imagery sessions, David became more comfortable with the idea of accidentally causing the death of bugs and his therapy shifted to his fear of hitting pedestrians. During treatment, David was asked to imagine that he was driving on a crowded road lined with houses, with people crossing the street. Suddenly he feels the car hit a bump. He wonders if it is actually a bump or a person. He decides not to stop and check but to drive away. As he continues on his way, a police car comes behind him with lights and siren. He is stopped for hit-and-run driving because he has hit and killed a man who was a father to five children. As the story continues, David goes through a trial in which he faces the widow, who confronts him with the consequences of his irresponsible driving. David was asked to listen daily to a forty-five-minute tape of this fantasy until his distress level decreased considerably.

Finally, the most fearful images were introduced, which described him dropping his daughter on the concrete floor, causing her death. As this scene unfolds, his wife and his parents are at the funeral, accusing him of killing his daughter, and his father tells him, "We always knew you were an irresponsible person."

Simultaneously with this imagery practice, David was asked to confront actual situations that triggered his urge to check. This included flushing the toilet without checking to see if there were bugs in it, going to bed without checking the doors and windows, and leaving the kitchen after turning on the oven.

Many people have little concern regarding leaving an oven on an automatic timer while at work, but David struggled with the task as though he were lighting a torch to his house. During special sessions held in David's home, he turned on his stove, turned on faucets and left them dripping, and then left the house for a half-hour walk with his therapist.

During some treatment sessions, David drove his car with the therapist as passenger. He was instructed to refrain from looking in the rearview mirror or checking in any other manner and to drive only once down any particular road. (At first David did not feel anxious when driving with the therapist and not checking, because he mentally assigned responsibility for any disasters to the therapist. He reasoned that if he actually hit someone, the therapist would never allow the victim to bleed to death. Such a mental strategy defeated the therapeutic purpose of the practice. So in future driving sessions with David, the therapist kept his eyes closed.)

Exposure was also introduced for David's fear of dropping his daughter. David carried his daughter back and forth across concrete floors for extended periods of time, especially when she was asleep.

After the three-week treatment, David began to function normally again. Three years later, at his last follow-up review, he reported that his checking lasted about five or ten minutes a day. This involved making sure the windows and doors at work were locked, since he was the last person to leave the office each day, and ensuring that his front gate and front door were locked securely at night. David felt that this checking was not exaggerated, and he was satisfied with the results of his treatment.

MIKE Mike was a thirty-seven-year-old accountant who suffered from checking rituals from the age of sixteen. Most of his concerns were typical of checkers. When at home, he spent a great deal of time in his kitchen, checking the stove and electrical appliances. He also checked to make sure lights were off throughout the house. And before leaving the house he carefully checked and rechecked doors and windows. Checking the front door alone before he went to work each morning involved a half-hour ritual.

Leaving his car also triggered Mike's urge to check. He had to make sure the lights were off, the hand brake was on, the windows were closed, the doors locked, and the gearshift was either in first gear when the car was facing uphill or reverse when it was downhill. This routine usually required twenty minutes. Mike wanted to make sure no children could get into the car, start it, and then accidentally kill themselves and others. So between leaving the house in the morning and leaving his car in the parking lot, Mike spent close to an hour in checking rituals. Inevitably he was late for work, which produced numerous added problems.

When asked to list his concerns and rank them in order of how distressing they were, Mike presented the following list:

Leaving the house, without checking the lights,
   for half an hour: 40
Leaving the car for five minutes without checking: 55
Leaving the kitchen without checking the
   stove and electrical appliances: 65
Leaving the house for work, checking
   the door only once or twice: 85
Leaving the car in the parking lot for an
   entire day, checking everything only once: 95–100

For checkers, exposure automatically includes ritual prevention. (If you don't prevent the checking, there is no purpose in practicing exposure.) Mike's treatment included leaving each situation after checking only once or not checking at all, then half an hour later coming back and repeating the process. Thus, Mike learned that disaster did not occur when he neglected to check the doors and windows of his home, or his car windows and brakes.

At the same time Mike was gradually learning to leave situations without checking more than once, the therapist asked him to create five scenes describing catastrophes he feared would happen if he did not check properly. In the first scene, Mike imagined he deliberately decides not to check the stove and electrical appliances. This causes the house to catch on fire and burn down because the fire department doesn't arrive on time. The second scene involved leaving the house without checking doors and windows because he decides, at the expense of his view of being responsible, to get rid of his OC symptoms. A burglar enters the house while he is gone and takes all the family's valuable, uninsured possessions. His wife chastises him, his parents feel ashamed of him, and his family suffers financial hardship. A third scene involved leaving the car without checking. A child gets into the car, releases the brake, and is seriously injured when the car hits a tree. The child's parents arrive at the hospital and accuse Mike of harming their child.

Five years after his three-week program, Mike continues to enjoy his life with his family and has become more successful in managing his accounting business. He experiences some difficulty with his car; he still needs to check it for about five minutes before he can leave it for the day. The remainder of his obsessions and rituals have disappeared.

RICHARD The treatment of Richard, the checker discussed in Chapter 2 who feared writing "I'm a fraud" on his checks, was straightforward. It consisted of exposure and ritual prevention. Since he worried every time he considered writing a check, regardless of where he was, much of his treatment took place in the therapy office.

Treatment consisted of asking Richard to write checks to a whole host of people, then signing them "I am a fraud" instead of his name. In this case, part of his feared disaster actually came true. The therapist asked him to place each check in an envelope, address it to the designated person, and give the sealed envelope to the therapist. He was to turn over all the envelopes without knowing what the therapist would do with the checks.

Richard assumed that the therapist would not actually mail those checks, but at the same time he wasn't certain he would get them back. So in his mind those checks were floating around, no longer in his possession. They could get lost or mailed accidentally. These thoughts, which occurred during the treatment sessions, stimulated his obsessions and forced him to confront his worst fears. By the end of his three-week treatment, Richard was practically free from all his obsessions and compulsions.

NANCY Let's see how these principles are applied in the treatment of repeaters, such as Nancy. As you may remember from Chapter 2, Nancy used to dress and undress herself hundreds of times a day in order to protect members of her family from dying in an accident. In treatment the therapist asked Nancy to produce the thought "Oh, my God, what will happen if my husband is now in an accident?" and then sit quietly and contemplate the possibility that her husband had indeed died in an accident. She was asked to imagine that it was her fault. She could have saved him by dressing and undressing, but she was so focused on taking care of herself and trying to get rid of her ritualistic behavior that she allowed him to die. During these treatment sessions, of course, Nancy was prevented from dressing and undressing. After repeated exposure to these images, Nancy could think about her family being involved in an accident without experiencing the urge to dress and undress.

The Treatment of Hoarders and Orderers

Hoarders and orderers do not often seek treatment because, for the most part, they do not perceive their rituals—hoarders collect objects and orderers arrange them—as posing undue inconvenience. However, the symptoms often inconvenience their family and friends. For instance, orderers may constantly reprimand their children for moving household items out of the prescribed order. Likewise, hoarders may fill their homes with junk, crowding family members. Often the families of hoarders and orderers pressure them into getting treatment.

Rituals for hoarders and orderers are triggered when they notice particular items not in place or not yet part of their collection. Their treatment program involves confronting those situations and practicing ritual prevention. If you are a hoarder or an orderer and want to get rid of your symptoms, you will realize, after reading Donna's case, that you can easily devise your own self-help program.

DONNA Donna, mentioned in Chapter 2, had both hoarding and ordering rituals, so her case can exemplify how both are treated. Treatment took place mostly at her home. The therapist elaborately disorganized her entire apartment so that Donna couldn't find most of the things she wanted. In Donna's case, her main fear was that she would not be able to tolerate the distress caused by a disorganized home. However, by the end of three weeks of exposure to a disordered apartment, her distress diminished and she was not disturbed anymore by clutter. At that point, she was no longer afraid of visitors coming to her home, since their potential disruption of order did not alarm her.

The treatment for her hoarding behavior was delayed for four days to allow Donna to become accustomed to a disorganized apartment. As you will remember, hoarders worry that they will later need a specific object but will not have it because they have discarded it. It is nearly impossible to generate a treatment that proves they won't need an object, since in their mind it might be years before they actually need it. Instead, they must adopt the attitude that no disaster will occur if they do not have the object. By doing so they will be able to accept the risk that one day, ten years from now, they actually will need that special article they threw out years ago. This learning occurs through habituation: The longer they spend directly facing their anxiety, the less anxious they become.

In the beginning Donna was horrified by the thought of throwing out things and of not hoarding anymore. So in this phase of treatment, the therapist sat next to Donna in her home and helped her throw away some of the collections she had kept for years. They started with the paperbacks, since they were the least important to her, and ended with magazines and newspapers. After three weeks of this regimen, habituation had occurred, and Donna felt only slight distress while throwing out things. She was still uncertain whether she would need part of her collection in the future but could tolerate this uncertainty. The experience of discarding objects no longer terrified her.

The Treatment of Thinking Ritualizers

Treatment involving ritual prevention works better with rituals such as checking, washing, or ordering than with thinking rituals. This is because a behavioral ritual can be more readily controlled than a thinking ritual can. For example, you can have the urge to wash yet can stay away from a faucet and not wash until the urge dissipates. You can also ask for help to distract yourself if the urge becomes very strong. In fact, therapists encourage patients to choose a support person who will stay with them during treatment and distract them when the urge becomes extreme. However, with thinking rituals, such as praying, repeating words, or repeating numbers, the obsessive-compulsive has much less self-control. Even with the best intentions, OC's report that the rituals often surface in their minds automatically.

Specific instructions may prevent such compulsions. These include immediately stopping the repetitious thought as soon as you become aware of it. You then purposely bring an obsessive thought back into your mind. In response to this negative thought, you will again feel compelled to begin repeating a "good" thought. Yet, this time you purposely refrain from such a compulsion. This way, even if you accidentally start your obsession, you have an opportunity to practice ritual prevention.

An example is Bob, described in Chapter 2, who repeatedly prayed for forgiveness in case he might have insulted other people. When he noticed himself spontaneously praying in a ritualistic manner, the therapist asked him to think immediately about a situation in which he insulted someone. Instead of praying, he was instructed to think "Well, that's the way it is. I have insulted someone, and I will have to take the consequences." Bob was then to imagine how hurt and angry the other person was. This gave him a chance to face his distress instead of reducing it by praying.

Another helpful technique for preventing thinking rituals, further described in the next chapter, is to write down the obsessional thoughts or to vocalize them over and over again for a prolonged period of time. The act of writing or reciting is incompatible with engaging in thinking rituals and thus diminishes the likelihood they will occur spontaneously. The addition of writing and vocalizing practice to Bob's treatment helped him overcome his thinking rituals.

The examples we have described illustrate the most successful professional therapy known for obsessive-compulsive ritualizers. The therapist helps you when you devise and begin practicing your own self-help program, as outlined in the next chapter.

8 🍂

YOUR THREE-WEEK
SELF-HELP PROGRAM

THIS CHAPTER WILL help you, step by step, to devise your
personal Three-Week Program. We will begin by explaining
what you need to prepare for such an intensive undertaking,
and offer general guidelines for starting your program. Next,
we will outline five specific programs for the major rituals:
washing and cleaning, checking and repeating, ordering,
hoarding, and thinking rituals. At the end of the chapter we
will explain how to make adjustments to your program if you
suffer from more than one type of ritual. We will also teach
you how to respond to setbacks during your progress and how
to continue to control your symptoms after you have finished
the program.

The self-help program described requires strong determination and commitment from the start. This is the moment to
pause, look carefully into yourself, and ask, "Am I *really* ready
to get rid of my symptoms? Am I willing to invest considerable
time and effort during the next three weeks in order to regain
control over my life?" As the recovered obsessive-compulsives
will tell you in Chapter 10, this is an extremely effective
program, but it will only work if you are ready. It is important

that you not start the program until you are fully committed to experience at least ten days of intense discomfort. On occasion you may have to practice your skills continually for eight or ten days straight before you begin to notice your distress diminishing. As it does, your urge to ritualize will become easier to resist.

The Three-Week Program provides an opportunity for you to learn that you *can* control your obsessions and compulsions. The more often and the longer you expose yourself to the situations that distress you, the faster you will gain freedom from your symptoms. Take advantage of every opportunity that comes your way for confronting your worries and obsessions, and learn to break your well-established habit of avoiding these situations.

Keep in mind that the first few days of the program are the most difficult ones, and even these days may not be as difficult as you imagine them to be. This was the experience of many of the sufferers included in Chapter 10. For most OC's, the first few days are quite hard, and they need all the help and support they can get.

Preparing for Your Self-Help Program

As you have probably already guessed, the program will become the center of your life for three weeks. You need to prepare your environment carefully to maximize the benefits. Here are several suggestions you can follow:

1. *Rearrange your daily commitments.* The Three-Week Program will consume a great deal of your time. You will need to reduce outside activities that are part of your life-style. You may even find it useful to take a vacation from work and arrange for child care.

2. *Prepare your family and friends.* Your family or friends

may have become a central part of your obsessions and rituals. If you are a washer, perhaps you worry not only that you will become sick from contamination, but also that your children and spouse will catch a disease. You might be afraid that they, being not as careful as you are, will contaminate the house and thereby cause you discomfort and illness. If so, you probably have tried to control their behavior as well as your own. Many washers ask their children to wash their hands more often than necessary, request that their spouses leave their street shoes outside the door, or restrict their children from bringing friends home.

There are other ways you might involve your family in your symptoms. Perhaps you, as many washers do, repeatedly ask others to reassure you that you washed or cleaned enough or that you did not touch a contaminant. Such requests aggravate your problem and will need to stop.

Obviously, the Three-Week Program cannot succeed without the agreement of family members to help you by changing some of the ways they have been responding to your symptoms. Specifically, you and your family need to adopt the following guidelines:

- *Family members should stop helping you perform your rituals.* For example, spouses should refuse to check doors and electrical appliances repeatedly or keep track of the number of times you rotate your hands while washing.
- *Family members should stop performing any rituals because of your obsessions.* You should instruct your children to refuse your requests to wash excessively or to take their temperature repeatedly. If your children are young, your spouse should be in charge of routines that have been the focus of your compulsions.
- *Family members must agree that your requests for reas-*

surances will not be granted. When you ask questions such as "Did I touch the toilet seat?" "Do I have a lump on my neck?" or "Should I call the Poison Control Center?" your family should respond by saying, "We have all agreed that we cannot answer this question."

Whether you live with your spouse and children, with your parents, or with a friend, follow the above guidelines. If you are living alone, think about whether you involve certain individuals in your rituals or seek reassurance from them. If the answer is yes, we advise that you inform them about your planned program and review the preceding guidelines with them.

3. *Choose supportive people to help you practice.* During the Three-Week Program, you are likely to become quite distressed at times, especially when you feel strong urges to ritualize. Be sure to elicit help from a supportive family member or close friend who understands your problems and realizes the demands of this program. A supportive and encouraging relationship will make those distressing times easier to bear. Often one person cannot be available at all times, so you might want to involve others in this role.

It is important that you share the details of the program with your support people and clarify their responsibilities. These should be written down and provided for each person involved in your practice. If possible, arrange the exact time your support people will be available to help you each day. Each should be able to devote a minimum of two hours per day throughout the three-week period to help you practice.

Consider these guidelines for selecting your support people:

- They should be warm and encouraging.
- They should be ready to suggest and participate in activities—taking a walk, engaging in conversation, shopping, or going to the movies—that will distract you from the urge to ritualize.
- They should not use force or ridiculing comments if they find you engaging in your rituals. Instead, they should remind you of your commitment and help you engage in distracting activities.
- As with family members, other support people should not reassure your obsessive concerns or help you perform your rituals.

The Three Techniques of Your Self-Help Program

In the previous chapter we discussed three parts of the treatment program for obsessive-compulsive ritualizers. You will be using these same techniques in your self-help program, so let's briefly review them. The first is *exposure*. This means simply that you will directly confront the situations that cause you distress, anxiety, shame, disgust, or other negative emotions. You need to face situations that provoke your urge to engage in compulsive actions.

The second part of this program is *imagery practice*. This means you will imagine circumstances you fear will happen if you have not ritualized enough (you identified such images in Chapter 3). During exposure and imagery practice, your distress will gradually diminish as you get used to confronting your fears. We call this process *habituation*.

The third part is *ritual prevention*. This means that as you follow the program you will not engage in the compulsive behaviors you listed in Chapter 3. The instructions about ritual prevention vary from one ritual to another. We will outline them as we present the self-help programs for each specific ritual.

It is important that you include in your self-help program all three procedures: exposure, imagery practice, and ritual prevention. Studies conducted at the Center for the Treatment and Study of Anxiety at the Medical College of Pennsylvania show that all three parts are essential for your success. We have found that people who engage in only one of these procedures had little improvement and the improvement they had usually did not last.

GUIDELINES FOR EXPOSURE AND IMAGERY PRACTICE Below you will find ten guidelines to help you with your exposure and imagery practice:

1. Start by turning back to Tables 1 and 2 in Chapter 3 (pages 56 and 58) and review the situations and thoughts that provoke your distress.
2. Begin your program with situations that evoke a discomfort rating of about 50. As the program progresses you will gradually proceed upward to the items that provoke your highest discomfort level.
3. Each time you practice, confront a given situation or image until your discomfort level decreases by at least half.
4. Practice again and again with each given situation or image until your discomfort decreases significantly. At that time you can proceed to the next highest item on your list.
5. Practice daily, with sessions lasting at least one or two hours. Studies have repeatedly found that long exposures are much more effective than short ones. Therefore, it is best that your exposure be continuous and not interrupted. If you confront a distressing situation in

time segments of five minutes each, your distress will not decrease much, even if your total exposure time is one or two hours. So make sure your exposure practice is continuous. The rule of thumb: Do not end an exposure practice until your discomfort is reduced at least by half.

6. Use Tables 9 and 10 on pages 161 and 162 to monitor each exposure practice. Write down the situation, object, or image you practiced that day and monitor your distress level periodically.

7. If your discomfort with a situation or image does not decrease during any given day, then practice this situation an extra day and, if possible, add another hour to your exposure practice.

8. Once your distress level stays consistently low over several days with a particular situation or thought, you need not continue practicing it regularly.

9. Continue the program until you have successfully confronted the most distressful situations or images on your list. If you do not confront the situations that evoke the highest distress, it is more likely you will lose the gains you made during the program.

10. Enlist the help of supportive friends or relatives whenever you feel that such help is going to encourage you to work harder.

Special Guidelines for Imagery Practice. There are three circumstances when imagery practice will be of special help. The first is when you want to confront the disasters you imagine will happen if you don't ritualize enough. If you can't create a direct exposure that will elicit those images and thoughts, then you will need to design an imagery practice. A second reason for using imagery is if the situation that distresses you is not readily available for exposure. For example, if you feel contaminated by a specific apartment in a town where you no longer live, it will be helpful to practice by imagining yourself in that apartment (although your program must eventually include a visit to such a place). The third reason for using such imagery is to prepare you for exposure. Some people who are extremely afraid to confront an actual situation find it helpful to first practice being there in their imagination.

When you are ready to begin imagery practice, here are the guidelines to follow. Find a tape recorder and a blank audio-tape of at least forty-five minutes' length. We recommend a portable tape player with an earphone, since it allows you to move about while practicing. Review Table 3 in Chapter 3 (page 59). Pick the five most distressing circumstances from that list of eight. Begin with the least distressing of the five and write a four- or five-page story about that consequence. You will find it easier to write this story if you imagine you are actually in a situation likely to lead to this catastrophe. Imagine you are in the scene and decide not to ritualize. Now write your story about what terrible events will occur next. An example of one woman's story is given on pages 159–60.

You are now ready to record your story. Read it several times carefully; think about the details. Then close your eyes and imagine that the story you have written is actually happening now. Turn on your tape recorder and tell the story into the microphone in the present tense. Do not read directly from your written pages. Remain with your eyes closed and describe in detail exactly what happens in your story: what is happening around you, what actions you are taking, and what terrible disasters are happening to you and to others around you because you have not ritualized adequately.

THE STEPS OF IMAGERY PRACTICE

1. Review the five most distressing circumstances from Table 3 in Chapter 3.

2. Write an explicit, detailed (four- to five-page) story of the least distressing of these five consequences.
3. Record this story on an audiotape.
4. Listen to this tape twice in a row (about forty minutes) each day until it no longer evokes significant anxiety.
5. Then repeat this same process for the next-highest negative consequence on your list.

The more details you include in the story, and the more you describe exactly how upset you are, the more likely this procedure will help you. Become involved in the story and imagine it's real. In this way, when listening to it later you will be more likely to become as distressed as you would in the actual situation. And this is the goal: to make certain you feel distressed while listening to the tape. By doing so you will habituate to your catastrophic images and thoughts, and they will diminish.

Before starting the recording, set a timer for twenty minutes so that you can concentrate on imagining your story and recording it without worrying about the time. Listen to this tape for at least forty minutes per day, every day, until it evokes very little distress in you. Once that occurs, proceed to your next-most-distressing circumstance and follow these same instructions.

EXAMPLE OF AN IMAGERY SCRIPT FOR A WASHER

I am sitting here in the chair. The door opens and my mother comes in. She enters the room, she sees me, and she says, "I'm glad to see you. It's been a long time." She comes to me, and she touches me. She wants to hug me. My mother is astonished that I let her hug me, and she says, "I can't believe that I am allowed to hug my daughter again." Now I feel the contamination spreading all over me. I can feel her hands on my back. And I begin to feel that the contamination will never go away.

It can never be washed off. I would like my mother to leave, and I want to take a shower or a bath so I can feel clean again. I can't say anything. I can't move; I am overwhelmed by the feeling of being contaminated. My mother is standing beside me, and she is holding my hand and I can feel how she becomes even more contaminating. I would like her to take her hand away. She is asking me, "Are you afraid of me?" and I would like to explain to her how much afraid of her I am, but I don't say anything. I just let her hold my hand and let her hug me. I let her sit beside me, very close, and she is contaminating me. I can feel the contamination all over my body. I wish I could run out and scream and never come in contact with her again. Yet, I stay here, I stay beside her as she contaminates me more and more. I feel the burning spots on my back and hands. It is the feeling of contamination, creeping up my arms, creeping up my face—it's all over my body.

I try to keep my arm still to make sure that the parts that are not contaminated now will remain clean. But it is spreading over my whole body. My mother is still beside me, still contaminating me. She is contaminating me more and more. She is telling me something, but I can't really listen to her. I am so upset, my heart is beating, I can feel my heart beating really fast. I feel as though I am going to faint. Yet, something forces me to stay and listen to her. I would like to run to the next room, but I realize I have to face the fact that I can't avoid my mother any longer. I feel trapped. She will never go away, she will go on contaminating me forever, more and more. I will never feel free again. I have the urge to leave the room and to forget everything about my mother. But her touch is everywhere on my body.

Keeping a Record of Your Exposure Practice. It is a well-known fact that feedback helps a person learn a new skill.

Therefore, it is important that you constantly monitor your progress during practice. Tables 9 and 10 are designed to make this task easy for you.

Use Table 9, which follows, when you practice exposure. Here you are asked to rate your distress level initially, five minutes later, and then every ten minutes for the first forty-five minutes. Thereafter, rate your distress every fifteen minutes.

TABLE 9:
DISTRESS LEVELS DURING EXPOSURE

Date_____   Day Number_____

Initial Distress Level (0–100)_____

Initial Urge to Ritualize (0–100)_____

Description of Exposure_____

During the Practice Session, Rate Your Distress Level (0–100):

Initial Distress Level_____	At 1 hour_____
At 5 minutes_____	At 1 hr. 15 min._____
At 15 minutes_____	At 1 hr. 30 min._____
At 25 minutes_____	At 1 hr. 45 min._____
At 35 minutes_____	At 2 hours_____
At 45 minutes_____	At end of session_____

Table 10, coming up, is designed to help you monitor your progress during imagery practice. Notice that on this form we only ask you to make three ratings. This is because we do not want you to rate your distress during imagery; it may interfere with your concentration on the imagery and thereby reduce the effectiveness of the practice. At the end of each imagery practice, fill out the form. Recall to the best of your ability how distressed you were in the first five minutes, what your highest level of distress was during the practice, and how distressed you were at the end. Write these three numbers on the form using a 0 to 100 scale.

TABLE 10:
DISTRESS LEVELS DURING IMAGERY PRACTICE

Date_____   Day Number_____

Initial Distress Level (0–100)_____

Initial Urge to Ritualize (0–100)_____

Description of Imagery_____

_____

At the End of the Session, Rate Your Distress Level:

During first five minutes_____

At peak_____

At end_____

Self-Help Program for Washing and Cleaning Rituals

If you have concerns about contamination that lead to washing and cleaning rituals, the best self-help approach to take is exposure and ritual prevention.

HOW TO DESIGN YOUR EXPOSURE Review the list of the ten most distressing situations you identified on Table 1 in Chapter 3 (page 56). Use this list as a plan for your program.

On *Day One* follow these three steps:

Step 1. Start by locating the situation or object you rated as "about 50" on your list (moderately distressing). Place your hands on the contaminating object or surface. You might find this experience quite distressing. But don't remove your hands until you begin to experience significant reduction in discomfort or until your practice time is completed. You may want to use the exposure time to practice your brief relaxation skills— the Calming Breath and the Calming Counts—that were presented in Chapter 5 (page 91). Another way to help yourself tolerate the distress is to carry a card with you on which you've written the following two things:

1. Anxiety does not remain forever. As I continue to stay in the situation, my anxiety will diminish.
2. The chance that I will get harmed by this action is negligible.

As you begin, keep in mind that you may not experience immediate improvements. Some people need several hours of exposure before they notice a change in their reactions; others need a few days. Just stick with your practice and you too will turn the corner on your discomfort.

Step 2. Now place your hands in your hair and on your face, arms, and legs. In short, contaminate yourself all over your body. Spreading contamination in this manner will probably increase your distress. *Keep in mind that your distress will diminish.* Continue to contaminate your body until you are significantly less distressed, about 30 to 40 on your distress scale.

For some people, anxiety will not diminish significantly in the practice periods of the first few days. If this is true for you, simply begin again at Step 1 each day.

Step 3. Whether or not you experience significant reduction of distress during these first two steps, proceed to contaminate your living environment. If you are practicing at home, walk through all the rooms of your house, touching objects in each room. It is especially important to contaminate the sofas and chairs you usually use. Also, contaminate your bed sheets and pillows so you stay in contact with contaminants throughout the night. If your contaminating object is something outside your home, such as the doorknobs of a store, then touch that object with a handkerchief, carry the handkerchief home, and use it to contaminate common objects throughout your house.

If your fear includes contaminating other people, then you must find a way to contaminate them during your exposure practice. Use a contaminated handkerchief to touch common areas of public places, such as counters of supermarkets and department stores. If you worry about contaminating specific individuals, like your spouse or children, you need to contaminate them in your daily practice.

Remember, the longer you stay in uninterrupted contact with the contaminant, the faster your worry will be diminished.

On *Day Two,* repeat Steps 1 through 3, using the same contaminant. If your distress has diminished considerably by the second day, proceed with Item 2 on your list (a rating of "about 60"), repeating Steps 1 through 3. While practicing on the new item, remain in contact with Item 1 by contaminating a handkerchief, towel, or paper with that object and putting it inside your pocket or pocketbook.

If you are still feeling highly distressed with Item 1, don't begin practice with Item 2. Instead, continue to practice with Item 1 using Steps 1 through 3.

On *Day Three,* first test your distress level for Item 1 and Item 2 by touching them. If your distress has decreased considerably for both items, stay in contact with them as just described and begin practicing with Item 3, following Steps 1 through 3. If your distress level is still high for Item 2, don't proceed to Item 3. Instead, practice with Item 2, following Steps 1 through 3.

On *Day Four,* test your distress level with Items 1, 2, and 3 by touching each. If all of them still cause great distress, devote most of your practice time to Item 3, but leave some time to practice with Items 1 and 2 as well. If your distress levels are low, start practicing with Item 4 by repeating Steps 1 through 3.

By *Day Five,* it is important that you are practicing with Item 4. *For the remaining days* of your program, progress through your list on Table 1. Continue to carry with you contaminants from all previous items. By *Day Thirteen* or *Fourteen* you should be confronting the highest item in your hierarchy.

If by *Day Thirteen* you have not experienced reduction in your distress level for any of the situations you have practiced, we recommend that you seek the assistance of a specialist in cognitive-behavioral therapy before you continue.

During *Days Fourteen* through *Twenty-one,* devote your practice time to the most distressing situations in your hierarchy. Often, those highly distressing situations require more practice before you experience significant relief.

During your program you may also discover distressing situations you had not previously noticed. Use this last week of the program to practice with these situations.

Your attitude during exposure practice will determine how successful you will be. Subtle avoidance reflects a reluctance to give up your symptoms completely and will hinder your progress. *Practice as much as you can. Seek opportunities to practice* in the course of your everyday activities. Whenever you detect your reluctance to confront a situation, take it as a signal that you must include this situation in your practice. Seeking opportunities to practice reflects your total commitment to getting rid of your symptoms.

Special Concerns During Exposure A common question raised by individuals who practice exposure is "How much of the contaminant must I touch in order to improve?" Suppose you worry that household chemicals will harm you or others, and you avoid using them because of this. You would want to know how much of the chemical you can safely contact during your exposure practice. The rule is *don't be concerned about small amounts*. For exposure to cleaners such as Endust and Liquid Comet, wet a paper towel slightly with them and contaminate yourself and your surroundings according to Steps 1 through 3.

Another group of common contaminants are bodily secretions, notably urine and feces. How much urine or feces should you spread on yourself or others? As a rule, contact with your own feces and urine is unlikely to harm you. But large amounts may feel repulsive, and it is not necessary to use a lot in your self-help program. The idea in exposure practice is not to smear your entire body with fecal matter but to have contact with enough of it so that you feel contaminated, and thus, over time, diminish this worry. A small residue of feces on toilet paper is usually enough to provide this effect.

To practice exposure to urine, get a small sample of your own. Following Steps 1 through 3, place a few urine drops on a paper towel and hold the towel with both hands until your distress has reduced by half. Then put the towel on your face, your head, and all over the clothes you are wearing. Rub the towel on your clothes, your underwear, the dishes, counters, and other important areas of the house. Again, it is not necessary for the towel to drip with urine. It is enough to use only several drops, as long as you believe the towel is contaminated.

Another question that often arises during an exposure program is "Why should I do something that people normally would not do?" For example, if you feel contaminated by bathrooms and toilet seats, it is important that you incorporate into your self-help program touching the seat, the rim, and the toilet water with your bare hands, following Steps 1 through 3. You may wonder why you must place your hands in a toilet when you wouldn't do it in the normal course of your day. The idea of exposure practice is to exaggerate contact with contaminants in order to successfully eliminate your obsessional worry about them. This calls for behaviors that are not common practice in people's daily lives.

IMAGERY PRACTICE FOR WASHING AND CLEANING RITUALS
It is our experience that washing and cleaning rituals can be successfully controlled by using only exposure and ritual prevention. However, as we mentioned earlier, if you find yourself terrified by the thought of confronting your most distressing situation, use imagery practice to prepare for exposure. Follow the guidelines for imagery practice on pages 158 to 159. Write a four- to five-page story that describes in detail the situation, your actions in the situation, and the disaster you imagine will happen if you don't wash or clean. Imagine the story as vividly as possible, as though it were happening now, and tape-record your description of it while you are imagining it.

Be careful not to use imagery practice to avoid actual exposure. Soon after you experience some reduction in distress using imagery, schedule an exposure practice.

RITUAL PREVENTION FOR WASHING AND CLEANING RITUALS
As mentioned earlier, studies have indicated that ritual prevention is absolutely necessary for successful and lasting control over OC symptoms. The following ritual-prevention program has been found to be the optimal one for washing and cleaning rituals when used simultaneously with exposure practice. It is essential to include it in your Three-Week Program; follow it as strictly as possible.

Week One. During the first three days of this week do not handle water: Do not wash your hands, do not take a shower, and do not clean objects with water. You must avoid touching water for such a long period in order for you to realize that both your sense of contamination and the urge to ritualize will diminish without washing or cleaning and that no disaster will occur. Use rubber gloves when it is absolutely necessary that you come in contact with water.

On the fourth day you may take a ten-minute shower. If you typically shower in a ritualistic way, then reverse your sequence. For instance, if you usually wash from your feet and proceed up to your head, then in this ten-minute shower start with your head. If you have difficulty taking a short shower, enlist the help of your support person to remind you when the ten minutes are over. Immediately after this shower, contaminate yourself with whatever object or situation you are currently using in your exposure practice.

Continue to refrain from hand washing and cleaning during this week, but take another ten-minute shower on Day Six, using the preceding guidelines.

Week Two. In the second week take a ten-minute shower every other day, but refrain from washing your hands or using water in any other way.

RITUAL-PREVENTION SCHEDULE FOR WASHING
AND CLEANING

Week One
- No hand washing or cleaning
- No touching of water
- One 10-minute shower on Day 4 and Day 6; change order of any shower ritual; immediately after shower, contaminate self again
- No hand washing or cleaning
- No other touching of water

Week Two
- One 10-minute shower every other day; change order of any ritual; immediately after shower, contaminate self again

Week Three
- Five 30-second hand washings daily, never after touching contaminated object or using toilet
- No cleaning
- One 10-minute shower daily; immediately after shower, contaminate self again

Week Three. During the third week you can take a ten-minute shower daily and do five daily hand washings of not more than thirty seconds each. Do not wash your hands for at least an hour after touching a contaminated object or using the toilet.

After the three-week program, continue to follow the washing instructions of Week Three for at least three months, but resume your usual housecleaning chores.

How to Overcome Common Problems Ritual prevention may interfere with some of your daily hygiene habits. Here are suggestions regarding three areas of common concern:

1. You may continue to brush your teeth as you usually do. Just be careful that your hands do not touch the water. You may want to wear gloves to help you do this.
2. Many OC's take exception to the instruction not to wash their hands after using the toilet. You might find it helpful to remember that many cultures do not subscribe to this habit, and yet they survive. Also, remember that you need to exaggerate your contact with contaminants during the self-help program. In order to eventually feel relaxed without washing or cleaning you need to experience long periods during which you do not wash. This involves not washing your hands after using the toilet. When your symptoms diminish and your new normal cleaning and washing habits are established, you

may choose again to wash your hands after using the toilet.

3. If you feel contaminated by feces and urine, wear gloves while using the toilet for the first week. This keeps you from having to face the highest contaminant prior to practicing with less disturbing situations. But remember, by Day Thirteen or Fourteen, and preferably before that, you should use the toilet without gloves and not wash your hands after that.

Self-Help Program for Checking and Repeating Rituals

Checking and repeating rituals are basically similar. Both are attempts to prevent disasters that sufferers imagine will happen if they don't ritualize properly. The difference is that checking rituals are triggered much of the time by situations or activities. Repeating rituals, on the other hand, are triggered by thoughts, images, or impulses. Consequently, if you are a checker, your three-week program should include more exposure practice. If you are a repeater, you might need to use imagery practice more extensively.

EXPOSURE, IMAGERY PRACTICE, AND RITUAL PREVENTION In Chapter 3 you listed situations, thoughts, and images that produce your urge to check or repeat. In that chapter you also listed the disasters you fear will happen if you do not ritualize adequately. Use Tables 1, 2, and 3 (pages 56, 58, and 59) to design your three-week program.

A program for checking or repeating rituals is not structured to the same degree as a program for washing rituals. You may find it more difficult to distinguish between situations or thoughts that produce moderate anxiety and those that trigger intense distress. You need not worry about this. Start with any situation, thought, or image that typically provokes at least moderate distress.

Also, the distinction between exposure and ritual prevention is not as clear-cut for checking and repeating rituals as it is for washing rituals. Therefore we will describe the use of the two simultaneously. Because the guidelines for designing these programs are less rigid, we will outline several examples of programs for checking and repeating rituals.

CHECKING DURING DRIVING Suppose you are concerned about driving your car and hitting someone on the road. As a result, you repeat your route again and again to check for possible injured or dead bodies. You also check the tires when you come home, to detect signs of blood. You listen to the news and read the newspaper to find out if a hit-and-run accident was reported to the police. Your exposure program would be as follows:

Day One. Have someone drive you to a relatively quiet road with no pedestrians. When you arrive, get into the driver's seat, and ask your support person to close his (or her) eyes so you will not be able to rely on him for detecting injured persons. Drive half an hour to an hour on quiet roads until your distress is significantly reduced.

Day Two. Repeat this practice using a somewhat busier road.

Day Three. Repeat the drive on your Day One road alone instead of with your support person.

Day Four. Repeat the drive on your Day Two road alone.

Day Five. With your support person, go to the main street of the nearest small town. Drive through the downtown streets. Ask your support person to keep his eyes closed while you practice.

Day Six. Repeat your Day Five practice alone.

If you fail to experience a significant reduction in your distress level on any particular day, allow an extra repetition of that practice during the next day and postpone your next level of practice by one day. Continue to practice driving on busy streets until you feel comfortable.

While practicing your exposure program you may notice that you constantly worry about such matters as "What if I just hit a person, he is bleeding to death, and I could save him if I go back and check?" or "If I don't go and check, and the person I hit is dead, I will be charged with being a hit-and-run driver." We encourage you to *engage in these thoughts,* both during exposure and in between practices. In essence, when you focus on these thoughts, you are doing imagery practice in a natural manner. Some people find themselves thinking "I'm going to drive in the car and not worry about what happens" or "I'm sure that if something happens, my support person will tell me." If you have such thoughts you prevent yourself from being fully in touch with your distress.

If you avoid disastrous thoughts, we suggest that you add imagery practice to your program. Follow the guidelines for imagery on pages 157 to 159. Write a four- to five-page story that includes details of your catastrophe. An example: You are driving in heavy traffic, you have decided not to check, you have actually hit a person, fatally injured him, he dies, and you are caught by the police. You are brought to court, charged with being a hit-and-run driver. Your family sits in court with disapproving looks. It is all your fault.

Tape a detailed version of this story and listen to it repeatedly until your distress is significantly reduced.

By nature, exposure and ritual prevention for checkers always occur simultaneously. For instance, when you drive your route, you are practicing exposure, but since you are not repeating your route you are also preventing yourself from ritualizing. However, there are subtle ways you may still maintain some measure of avoidance or rituals such as quickly glancing at the mirror. Therefore, while you drive you need to follow these ritual-prevention instructions:

1. Do not use the rearview mirror during your drive. Glancing into mirrors is equivalent to checking and therefore should be avoided. If you need to change lanes, use your side mirror or quickly glance over your shoulder to verify that you are safe.
2. Do not drive on any road twice during the entire day's practice.
3. Do not check your tires when you come home.
4. Avoid listening to the news on the radio or TV and avoid reading the newspaper throughout the entire program.
5. Avoid asking family or friends reassuring questions.

CHECKING FOR SAFETY The most common checking rituals involve worry about one's home safety. It manifests itself in repeated checking of doors, windows, electrical appliances, cars, faucets, and light switches. Such checking rituals can be pervasive and involve hundreds of different activities per day. Doors and windows are checked to prevent a burglary or assault. Electrical appliances and outlets are checked to prevent fire. Cars are checked to prevent accidents.

If you have these types of worries and rituals, you may feel overwhelmed, asking yourself, "Where do I start?" You will find the following program we suggest to be a helpful model for devising your own program.

Suppose you find yourself checking the front door for an hour each time you leave the house. You check your windows for half an hour, check electrical appliances for ten minutes, and light switches for three minutes. In addition, you spend an hour checking these same things before you go to sleep. You also have difficulty leaving your car without repeatedly checking the hand brake, windows, doors, and lights. You spend fifteen minutes on those activities each time you leave the car.

We suggest you start with the most time-consuming rituals.

Day One. Before leaving the house, walk from one room to another. Glance once at each window, but don't check them again. You may check the electrical appliances, light switches, and faucets in your usual manner. Do not increase the time you spend on these items to make up for not checking the windows. Now leave the house. After locking the front door, verify it is locked by lightly pulling or pushing on the door handle. Then quickly get into your car and do an errand of at least one hour.

Repeat this sequence of actions four or five times today.

At night you can continue your regular routine, with the exception of the windows and front door. Do not check any windows tonight. After locking the front door, check that it is locked only by pushing or pulling on it lightly, one time.

Day Two. Stop checking your electrical appliances and outlets before leaving the house, and don't even glance at the windows. Leave the house in the same manner as you did on Day One. Tonight and each night from now on you may only check the front door by pushing or pulling on it one time lightly. Do not check any other items.

Day Three. Repeat your Day Two activities and also stop checking the light switches and faucets. On this day your primary assignment is to leave the house four or five times, for one hour each time, without any checking rituals.

Day Four. Continue your Day Three practice. Before leaving the house each time, turn on the oven. As you return, turn off the oven once without checking, and immediately leave the kitchen. Turn the oven back on as you leave the house again.

Each time you leave the house, drive away, park the car at a busy parking lot, and lock the doors. Once you're outside the car, check each door one time by pulling on its handle lightly, then walk away so you don't have a view of the car for at least half an hour.

Leave your house and leave your car four to five times today.

Day Five. Continue all the activities of Day Four. Add to them leaving two faucets in the house slightly dripping during each of your four or five outings.

Repeat this routine each day until you feel comfortable with it. You will probably start noticing that there are many other items in your daily routine that you check as well, such as making sure that the clock is far enough away from the edge of the table, that the freezer door is closed completely, or that you have written your checks correctly. Since by now you are not spending time with your main checking rituals, you can work on changing these other habits. Whenever possible, reverse your routines. Place the clock as close to the table's edge as possible without dropping it. Pull the food out to as close to the edge of the freezer as indicated safe by your support person. Write your checks as quickly as possible and mail them immediately.

During your program you will probably find yourself preoccupied with obsessions about your feared disasters. When leaving the house without repeated checking of the door and electrical outlets, you might think "What if somebody breaks in and steals the family's most valuable belongings, leaving us poor and needy?" or "What if the house catches fire, destroying all we have worked for?"

Don't try to push those thoughts away, even though they are distressing and painful. On the contrary, *dwell* on them as long and as vividly as possible. In this way you are doing imagery practice in the natural course of your day. If, on the other hand, you find you are pushing those thoughts away and dwelling only on your urges to ritualize, you need to structure imagery practice into your self-help program.

Follow the instructions for imagery practice on pages 157 to 159. Start by writing a four- to five-page story about your feared disaster. Record this story in detail on an audiotape and listen to it for forty-five minutes per day until you experience a significant reduction in your distress. Then move to a second scenario; create a story about your fear that your home might catch fire or that a child will enter your car, release the brake, and cause a serious accident because of your negligence in checking the doors.

GENERAL RULES IN A PROGRAM FOR CHECKING

1. Make a list of your major checking activities.
2. Start your program with preventing the ritual that is the least time-consuming and proceed gradually to the more time-consuming ones.
3. In the first week try to create gradual steps of exposure, starting with experiences that generate "about 50" on your distress scale.
4. Identify a specific ritualistic activity, and set a goal to stop it.
5. If you find yourself trying to avoid thinking about your feared catastrophes, schedule imagery practice.
6. Pay attention to your daily routine, and reverse any ritualistic habits.

REPEATING RITUALS Repeating rituals are often triggered by thoughts or images. Therefore, a program to overcome them should always include some imagery practice, although exposure and ritual prevention will be the focus. If you suffer from repeating rituals in order to protect yourself and your loved ones from being harmed, use the following example for devising your own three-week program.

Suppose you got the idea in your head that if you think about the name of your brother, Jim, or your wife, Jane, something terrible will happen to him or to her, such as a disease or death. You have stopped reading books or newspapers and avoided listening to the radio or TV for fear that you will encounter either of these names and thereby cause illness or death. These measures of protection are not sufficient, because in your mind your brother or wife can also die if you simply *think* about their names. And, of course, because you worry about them, you can't get their names out of your mind. You need additional ways of protecting them, and you gradually develop your ritualistic system. By ritualizing, you undo the thinking in the following magical way:

You have to repeat whatever action you were involved with at the moment you thought about the name. For example, if you were in the midst of drinking a cup of coffee, you have to put the cup down, bring it back up to your lips, and do it again and again until the thought disappears. You also count how many times you have repeated the action, because you consider the number *3*, its additions and its multiplications, as causing bad luck. So you have to make sure the number of times you repeat an action does not correspond to 3's.

Here is your program:

Day One. Write the names *Jim* and *Jane* on a pad continuously for forty-five minutes; listen for half an hour to a TV or radio show; and read the newspaper for half an hour, searching for the names Jim and Jane. At the same time, do not repeat any actions other than writing Jim and Jane on that pad.

Day Two. For forty-five minutes write the sentence "Jim and Jane will die because I am writing their names 3,333 times." Listen again to the TV or radio for half an hour and read the newspaper for half an hour in search of the names Jim and Jane.

Day Three. Get the book *Jane Eyre.* Skim through the book for forty minutes, noting the pages on which the name Jane appears. Write the name Jane 333 times. Keep the sheet of written names with you throughout the day. Look at it as often as you can. Continue your TV, radio, and newspaper assignment.

Day Four. Get the book *Treasure Island.* Follow the instructions for Day Three, using the name Jim instead of Jane. Continue your media assignment.

Day Five. Think about the name Jim or Jane while you engage in different types of activities, each activity in multiples of 3's. For example, think about the name *Jane* while you sit quietly on a chair. Get up while continuing to subvocalize the name *Jane.* Now repeat this process of sitting and standing nine times. Leave the chair and pick up the newspaper from the table. Think about the name Jim, and set the paper back down. Repeat this action three times. Think about the name Jim while you pass the threshold between the dining room and living room. Do this action six times. Continue with other such activities for a total of forty-five minutes. Also continue practicing your media assignment.

Proceed to engage yourself in situations that involve the names Jane and Jim while repeating actions in multiples of 3's until your distress subsides.

For the imagery practice in this program, refer back to pages 157 to 159. An example of a story is as follows: You have used the names Jane and Jim the wrong number of times, deliberately not protecting these people. They get sick with terminal cancer and soon die. It is all your fault. Your parents learn about what happened. They are very distressed and blame you for the deaths. If your obsession includes details of how Jane and Jim will become sick and die, then create this story and tape it. If your story is very short because your obsessions do not include a specific idea about how Jane and Jim die, then use a loop tape as described on page 95 in Chapter 4 and tape on it "Jim and Jane will die because I do not want to protect them."

Listen to the tape forty-five minutes per day until your distress subsides significantly.

GENERAL RULES IN A PROGRAM FOR REPEATING

1. Identify the thought, image, or impulse that triggers your compulsion.
2. Generate exposure practices that will include continuously repeating those thoughts and images, or writing them down repeatedly for thirty to forty-five minutes. Don't take breaks during this period.
3. Seek situations that will trigger your obsessions and confront them for at least thirty minutes each.
4. Pay close attention to your daily activities. Whenever you detect a reluctance to be in a situation or engage in an action, include that in your practice.
5. Detect any repeating patterns and reverse them. If you need to repeat actions seven times and avoid repeating three times, reverse that order. Repeat actions three times and avoid repeating them seven times.
6. Make use of imagery practice. If your obsessions are elaborate with details about the feared disaster, generate long tapes. If your obsessions include only short thoughts or images, create a loop tape. In both cases, practice imagery for forty-five minutes without breaks.

Self-Help Program for Ordering Rituals

The self-help program for ordering rituals is relatively simple, since most orderers do not imagine that terrible disasters will occur if their order is disrupted. If you suffer from ordering compulsions, you are likely to experience considerable distress when things are out of order. You probably believe that this distress will stay with you forever unless you restore the order. The three-week program aims at helping you realize that your distress will subside even though you don't order things in a ritualized manner. In general, a self-help program for ordering rituals focuses on exposure and ritual prevention. Only rarely does it include imagery practice.

Review Table 1 in Chapter 3 (page 56). Start with the situation that produces moderate distress ("about 50") and use the following example as a model for devising your own program. If you become distressed when your books are not lined up evenly, when your bedspread has one or two wrinkles, when your bric-a-brac have been moved from their exact spots, or when other people adjust your dining room chairs, take these steps.

Day One. Ask your support person to rearrange your books, making sure they are not lined up perfectly. Sit down and look at the bookshelves for twenty to forty-five minutes or until your distress has decreased considerably. Leave the shelves disorganized and come back to look at them four to five times during the day for at least ten minutes each time or until your distress diminishes.

Day Two. If you are still distressed about your disorganized books, schedule time to look at them for ten minutes four to five times per day. Ask your support person to unmake your bed and disorganize the drawers of your bureau. Have him or her keep the drawers part-way open. Do not change the appearance of your bedroom; then follow the instructions for Day One.

Day Three. Ask your support person to rearrange your den furniture in a way that would displease you. Leave it this way for the next two weeks. Leave the books, the bed, and the drawers in their disorganized state. Continue to disorganize your house in this manner until your distress diminishes.

After the end of the program, always leave some disorganized corners. Deliberately place things in a manner that displeases you. For example, if symmetry is important to you, create asymmetry. If you feel the left side of the curtains must exactly match the right side, make the two parts of the curtains unlike each other. If vases have to stand on the windowsill at exactly the same distance from the edge, deliberately rearrange them so that one is farther from the edge than the other. Then pay attention to those disruptions until you notice your distress has greatly subsided.

GENERAL RULES IN A PROGRAM FOR ORDERING

1. Identify "disorders" that cause you considerable distress.
2. Ask your support person to disorganize your home. Each day have him or her disorganize one room. Schedule four to five uninterrupted periods during the day to look at the disordered rooms. The lengths of such periods are flexible. Stay in each room until you experience considerable reduction in your distress.
3. Keep your house disorganized throughout the program.
4. Keep some corners of some rooms disorganized forever.

Self-Help Program for Hoarding Rituals

If you are a hoarder who is highly motivated to get rid of your collections, begin your program with imagery practice, following the instructions on pages 157 to 159. Write a four- to five-page story about the possible catastrophes that can happen to you because you discarded some article you now need.

For example, you collect newspaper articles because you are afraid that several years from now you will need one of these in order to discuss it with your friends. Eight years later you are at home having a dinner party. Someone starts a conversation about the greenhouse effect. You remember that several years ago you had read a very informative article about it. You get very anxious because you can't remember what was written in the article. You wish you had not thrown out your collections, so that you could refer back to the article and be a knowledgeable participant in the conversation. Instead, everyone else actively participates in the conversation, and you feel terrible because you know nothing. If only you had kept that article, people would not think you were ignorant. Make a tape of your story and practice imagery until your distress decreases considerably.

Now enlist the assistance of your support people. Set daily goals of what you want to throw out. This phase of the program is extremely difficult to accomplish alone. The help of your support people will ensure your progress. Continue to discard on a daily basis until you no longer own any needless collections.

GENERAL RULES IN A PROGRAM FOR HOARDING RITUALS

1. Start your program with imagery practice. Create several tapes.
2. Practice at least two hours per day by listening to your tapes. Try to imagine the events as vividly as you can, and try to become as distressed as possible.
3. Generate a list of your collections and decide which ones you will dispose of.
4. Enlist the assistance of your support people in setting up daily goals to throw away these collections.

Self-Help Program for Thinking Rituals

Thinking rituals are the most difficult to conquer because people have less control over their thoughts than their actions. If you suffer from thinking rituals, you can use ritual prevention by focusing continuously on your obsessional thoughts so that you don't have an opportunity to engage in subsequent thinking rituals. If, for example, you find yourself praying in a ritualized manner, using good numbers again and again to prevent a disaster, or thinking good thoughts to "undo" bad thoughts, follow the guidelines below to design your own Three-Week Program.

GENERAL RULES IN A PROGRAM FOR THINKING RITUALS

1. Generate a tape for your imagery practice by following the guidelines on pages 157 to 159. Create a four- to five-page story detailing the disasters that will occur if you do not undo your obsessional thoughts through thinking rituals. If, for example, you worry that you have insulted somebody and you pray compulsively for forgiveness, your tape might include the story of how rude you were to your boss, how you hurt his feelings, how he tells your coworkers about the incident, and about how everyone thinks you are an unworthy person. Listen to the tape in the manner described on page 159.
2. Create as many stories as you need to address your different obsessions.
3. Do not engage deliberately in your thinking rituals at any time.
4. If ritualistic thoughts begin spontaneously, do one of the following:
- Immediately stop the thoughts.
- Deliberately invoke the obsessional image or thoughts.
- Continue to think about the obsessional material until your distress has decreased considerably.

What If I Have More Than One Ritual?

Many obsessive-compulsives have more than one type of ritual. For most, however, one ritual dominates. First, identify your primary ritual by referring to Table 5 (page 62). Begin your program with this most frequent ritual, and devote the first week entirely to this ritual. If by the end of the first week you experience a great decrease in your distress and urge to ritualize, then in Week Two introduce your second-most-frequent ritual. Divide your practice time between the two rituals. If, however, by the end of the first week you still experience a considerable urge to ritualize, continue to work on your primary ritual until the middle or end of the second week. Then introduce the second ritual into your program. It is unlikely that you can successfully eliminate more than two rituals within three weeks unless they are minor and require little time and attention. If necessary, add one more week to your program to conquer your remaining symptoms.

Dealing with Setbacks

Even if you successfully follow the Three-Week Program, you may find that you have an occasional setback in which you notice a return of some of your symptoms. It is not easy to get rid of a well-established habit, and rituals are strong habits. Research has shown that 20 percent of those who participate in a cognitive-behavioral program lose some of their initial gains over the long run. This figure should not discourage you; it's much lower than the rate of relapse of those who quit smoking or those who lose weight. As with all habits, breaking patterns and establishing new ones requires continuous commitment and dedication.

There are usually three reasons why people have setbacks. The primary reason is not applying the follow-up program. So the best way to avoid a setback is to continue with the follow-up instructions for your particular symptoms. Take advantage of any opportunity to practice exposure. And whenever you begin to feel the urge to avoid, create a way to confront that situation.

Second, symptoms are more likely to return during stressful periods. If you begin to feel more pressure from work or from the responsibilities of home life or if someone close to you is sick or dies, these stresses can make you more vulnerable to your obsessive-compulsive symptoms.

Third, setbacks are more likely to occur with people who have not confronted all of their fearful situations within their original self-help program. This was true for Stephanie, who used checking behaviors to make sure things around her were safe. She confronted almost all of her fears through an exposure and ritual-prevention program and was able to bring her symptoms completely under control. Yet she refused to work directly on her fear that she might hit someone while driving. Instead, she chose to always drive with a passenger, who could reassure her that she had not hurt or killed someone.

For six months Stephanie functioned normally. Then, gradually, her symptoms returned. From this setback, however, Stephanie learned that she needed to reach the point where she *wanted* to give it *all* up, and until she reached this point there would always be something to hold her back.

So if you experience a setback, don't get discouraged. Discouragement often becomes a ticket for complete relapse. Instead, take a setback as an indication that you need to set up your original self-help program, work on it for a week, regain your ground, and proceed with the follow-up instructions.

Follow-Up Program

If you have followed the instructions for the Three-Week Program, you are likely to experience very little, if any, urge to ritualize. However, you may still notice some obsessional distress in certain situations or with certain thoughts. This distress will become less and less intense if you continue to follow the instructions for exposure, imagery practice, and ritual prevention.

A period of three weeks is long enough to break an old habit and to start adopting new habits. It is *not* long enough to completely rid oneself of old habits and solidly establish new ones. If you continue to follow the ritual-prevention instructions strictly, you will solidify your habits and they will become increasingly automatic.

Here are some further suggestions to help you maintain your gains.

FOR WASHING RITUALS

1. Take advantage of any opportunity in your everyday life to practice exposure. The more you continue your contact with previous contaminants, the faster you will get rid of residual distress.
2. Do not wash your hands more than five times a day, thirty seconds each time.
3. Do not use soap while washing your hands unless your hands are visibly dirty.
4. Hand washing should take place only after using the toilet, before handling food, or when hands are visibly dirty.
5. Take at most one ten-minute shower per day. Do not ritualize during the shower.

FOR OTHER RITUALS

1. For checking, do not check windows, doors, and the stove more than once when you leave home or before going to bed. Checking other items is prohibited.

2. For repeating, from time to time deliberately evoke thoughts or images that used to distress you, and refrain from repeating any actions.
3. For ordering, deliberately leave certain areas of your house slightly disorganized. From time to time, change the placement of decorative objects. Allow other people to make minor changes in the placement of objects and do not immediately rearrange them.
4. For hoarding, make a habit of throwing out unnecessary things on a daily basis.
5. For thinking rituals, from time to time deliberately evoke thoughts or images that used to distress you, and refrain from using thinking rituals.

What If I'm Not Making Any Progress?

The vast majority of obsessive-compulsives in a cognitive-behavioral program experience a gradual reduction in their obsessional distress and their urge to ritualize. A few do not. If you do not experience *any* improvement within two weeks, we suggest you consult a cognitive-behavioral therapist who specializes in OCD treatment. It is possible that you have misdiagnosed your problem and you do not have OCD. Or you may not have analyzed your symptoms correctly. Or perhaps anxiety or depression interferes with your ability to apply the self-help instructions. A professional consultation will help you clarify why you have not made progress.

9 ❦

MEDICAL TREATMENT

IF YOU HAVE been suffering from obsessive-compulsive disorder and have sought psychiatric help, you have probably tried a variety of medications, from the minor tranquilizers, such as diazepam (Valium), alprazolam (Xanax), and chlordiazepoxide (Librium), to antidepressant drugs like imipramine hydrochloride (Tofranil), amitriptyline hydrochloride (Elavil), or nortriptyline hydrochloride (Pamelor). In particular, antidepressants of all kinds have been prescribed for OC's, perhaps because many OC patients also suffer from moderate to severe depression. Although several drugs have been reported to help OCD symptoms in some individuals, for most there is little scientific evidence that these drugs have specific antiobsessive benefits. Three medications are currently receiving much attention from researchers studying the treatment of OCD. In this chapter we will briefly review these medications, then discuss when they might be useful.

Clomipramine (Anafranil)

The drug for OC symptoms that has been most researched today is an antidepressant called clomipramine (Anafranil), manufactured by Ciba-Geigy. In the 1970s, researchers began to notice that clomipramine was especially helpful for OCD and started to pay close attention to this drug. Recent studies have compared clomipramine with placebo pills and other antidepressants. The results of these studies showed a consistent picture: Clomipramine was the more helpful medication. About 50 percent of all OC's who received a therapeutic dose of clomipramine reported some benefits. Some showed moderate improvement while others found that their symptoms almost disappeared. In a large-scale study of several hundred patients in twenty-one sites, Ciba-Geigy reported that the average reduction of symptoms was 40 to 45 percent, using a daily therapeutic dosage of 100 to 250 milligrams of clomipramine.

Many patients describe their improvement in terms of their increased ability to tolerate their obsessions. Many report that they ritualize less and, although they may still obsess, they don't care as much about the fact that they are obsessing. When their OC symptoms cause less distress, it is easier for them to function in daily life. As they become more active, they can more easily tolerate their remaining obsessions or rituals. Although clomipramine rarely eliminates all symptoms, it is definitely helpful to many sufferers.

The therapeutic effects of antidepressants increase gradually over time. You may need to take clomipramine for four to six weeks before you notice any improvement, and twelve weeks before you gain the medication's full benefits.

Clomipramine, as all tricyclic antidepressants, can produce a variety of side effects, including dry mouth, dizziness upon standing, nausea, a drop in blood pressure, decreased mental alertness, drowsiness, sedation, fatigue, blurred vision, urination problems, and constipation. It can sometimes cause kidney problems and difficulty in reaching orgasm. We list these side effects here to educate you about the medication, not to scare you. Many people experience minor nuisance side effects, most of which diminish in a couple of weeks. Your physician will monitor your response to your medication, and you should disclose any side effects you experience. He or she will also recommend that you do not drink alcohol while taking an antidepressant.

Fluoxetine Hydrochloride (Prozac)

More recently two other new drugs have drawn attention as potentially helpful for OCD: fluoxetine and fluvoxamine. Fluoxetine hydrochloride (Prozac), a drug manufactured by Eli Lilly, is of greater interest for OCD sufferers because it is currently available in the United States. Clinical impressions of the usefulness of this drug are quite favorable. Early results indicate it might be as effective as clomipramine, but firm conclusions must wait until large-scale studies are completed. As with clomipramine, most patients who benefit from the drug still experience obsessions and compulsions, but these symptoms do not dominate their thoughts and actions. In other words, it is easier to dismiss an obsession and to resist a compulsion. The recommended dosage is from 20 to 80 milligrams per day.

Compared to other antidepressants, most patients find fluoxetine has fewer side effects. A common one is slight nausea, which for most people subsides over time. Unlike most antidepressants, it does not promote weight gain. On the contrary, it occasionally diminishes appetite. Other possible side effects include sleeplessness, constipation, agitation, tremors, weakness, and slowed movement. Alcoholic beverages should be avoided while taking this medication.

Fluvoxamine

Fluvoxamine is an antidepressant medication used in several European countries but is not yet approved for use in the United States. Several small-scale studies indicate that while taking this drug, 50 to 60 percent of patients improve moderately. The manufacturer is presently conducting a large-scale study in six cities around the country on the effect of this drug on OC symptoms.

The side effects associated with the use of fluvoxamine include nausea or vomiting, sleeplessness, agitation, decreased appetite, tremors, weakness, and slowed movement. As with all antidepressants, you should not drink any alcohol while you are taking fluvoxamine.

When Should Medications Be Taken?

As we indicated in Chapter 3, many OCD sufferers show some degree of depression. If you are severely depressed, you may find it difficult to generate the energy, commitment, and determination you need in order to begin a self-help program. One of the three medications described earlier may help by alleviating your depression and controlling some of your OC symptoms. Even if you experience great relief with medication (unless your physician specifically advises you against it), *it is important that you also use the self-help program.*

Medication may also help if you are so apprehensive about confronting your OC symptoms that you find yourself unable to practice your self-help skills. Here again, the medication might help reduce your symptoms to the extent that you will be able to begin your program. If you and your physician agree that medication might be helpful, then the ideal approach is generally to use the medication on a temporary basis in order to achieve a state of mind that will enable you to take full advantage of the self-help programs detailed for you in this book.

When you have established your new habits and gained control over your symptoms, medication usually can be withdrawn. One word of caution: If you decide to seek medication, find the help of a psychiatrist who is familiar with the specifics of medications for OCD. New research results are continually reported, and a specialist will keep abreast of the latest advances in this field.

Should Medication Be Used Instead of a Self-Help Program?

There are two reasons why we strongly encourage you to learn the self-help skills, even if the medication alone helps you. First, the long-term side effects of these medications are unknown. If there are approaches that help you control your symptoms without medication, the most prudent decision is to explore those options as well.

It is very likely that if you use medication alone to treat your OCD symptoms, when you stop the medication your symptoms will return. This is the second reason to pursue a self-help program.

The research on clomipramine illustrates this concern. When subjects stop taking the medication, their symptoms return. In a study conducted at the National Institute of Mental Health, more than 90 percent of the OCD patients who were placed on clomipramine had a complete return of their original obsessive-compulsive symptoms when the drug was withdrawn, irrespective of how long they had been taking it. It is as though the drug suppressed symptoms but did not eliminate them.

When you and your physician consider the use of medication, it is important to compare it to other treatment options.

In cognitive-behavioral therapy, the relapse rate is only 20 to 25 percent. In a recent study at the Center for the Treatment and Study of Anxiety at the Medical College of Pennsylvania, 90 percent of the patients showed significant gains after the three-week intensive program described in this book. One year later, 80 percent of those in the study still maintained their improvement—and these were patients with the most severe forms of the disorder. We expect that people with less severe symptoms will experience even greater, long-lasting gains.

10 ❦

GRADUATING FROM THE PROGRAM: ENCOURAGING STORIES FROM RECOVERED OBSESSIVE-COMPULSIVES

MANY OF OUR former patients were excited when they heard we were writing this book. They remembered how doubtful they were initially about being able to change their symptoms, and they wanted to carry a message of hope and encouragement to you by sharing their experiences.

You will hear how they used the same skills you have learned in this book to end the tyranny of OCD in their lives.

Listen for the different ways that these fellow sufferers found the strength to challenge their longstanding fears and avoidances. We hope that through their voices you will gain the courage and faith necessary to achieve your goals.

✻ Shirley

We will begin with Shirley, a fifty-two-year-old woman whose life was consumed by compulsions for almost forty-five years. Washing and repeating rituals dominated her adult life. Today, three years after completing the three-week intensive program, she reports being "ninety-five percent" symptom-free:

I can remember OCD symptoms back in first grade or even kindergarten. I didn't know what they were for a long time. The first compulsion I remember had to do with tying my shoes. After my mother would tie them I would yank them open and make her do them again and again until they felt tight enough. As a matter of fact, I still have the marks on my feet from having them tied so tight. Then I can remember the same thing with the barrette in my hair. It had to be just so tight that I could feel it.

I always had problems with water, whether it was bathing, doing the dishes, or washing my hands. Not to the extent of my problems as an adult, but there seemed to always be something in my mind about water. If I washed dishes I would have to have the water awfully hot, so hot that most other people couldn't even have touched it.

Then it just kept building and building. Sometimes I could take a shower and feel fairly normal. Then the next day I'd have all those crazy rituals again. I'd have to rinse this way or turn that way. I just could never understand why I could take a normal shower one day and then have problems the next.

Then it started building to other areas of my life. If I dusted the house then I'd redust and I'd dust again. If I had bought stock in Bounty paper towels I could probably retire by now! I just continuously used paper towels to do a lot of stuff. If I wet a towel and went over something, to me it was clean. Then I got to the point where I had to take the towels off the roll in a certain way. For instance, if I heard it coming off the roll or tore it off a certain way, it bothered me and I wouldn't use that piece. It was easy to go through a whole roll in just a short period of time.

I thought that if I didn't keep after these little things, they would close in on me and I wouldn't be able to touch anything. For example, there might be a little four- or five-inch spot on the floor that I would not touch in any way, shape, or form or place anything on. However, if I took my wet paper towel and wiped over it, it would be clean. In that way the rituals helped me.

I was a perfectionist, but I never knew what perfection was. So I could never really reach it. If I was making the bed, I would smooth and smooth and smooth the sheets, then walk away and be *drawn* back to continue smoothing the sheets until I got some kind of relief.

The hand washing started to get worse in my middle thirties. For example, going to the launderette became difficult. I would have to look at every machine, inside and out, for the cleanest one. Then I'd have to clean it more, with paper towels from the ladies' room. Once I got the clothes into the washer I would have to wash my hands. Sometimes I would be in the bathroom and think I would never get out. I was so petrified. I had the water splashing all over the place, and I was afraid people would hear me. I just couldn't get it right to get myself out. But somehow I always managed to. Then, when bringing the laundry home, if my husband set the basket in the wrong place, it would all be dirty to me and I'd have to do the entire laundry again.

As the years passed, I developed new rituals around repeating words and repeating other behaviors. While I dressed in the morning I had to comb my hair repeatedly in special areas. I had a lot of problems with the back of my head. I'd look in the mirror and comb quite a bit while doing little rituals. I used to say, "No, no, no." I didn't have a certain number of times I had to repeat the word *no*. I just said it until it felt OK to stop.

Most of the time I was in a hurry to get to work or to go someplace else. At those times I could say to myself, "I've got to go," and then I could break free.

I did similar things while I was washing my hands, too. I would do little things in the sink when I was washing. I'd say, "No, no," a lot. Then while I was moving my hands from one side to the other I began to count: one, two, three; one, two, three. I started the counting to get my mind off washing my hands, but that too became a habit.

Many, many things became rituals. When I was dressing I would button myself, then I'd have to open the buttons to make sure they were closed. And open them and close them and open them and close them. I did the same things with a zipper. When I was putting on a pair of slacks, if one leg brushed the floor and I thought that area of the floor was probably dirty, I would have to immediately take off the slacks and put them in the laundry basket.

Almost everything had a ritual to it, even putting the dishes in the dishwasher. I had to place them perfectly. I broke a lot of those spikes off in the dishwasher trays because if they weren't just so, sometimes I'd get frustrated and break them off purposefully. Or I'd twist them so much to have them in a perfect position that I would break them off. Sometimes I would wash the dishes two or three times because they didn't feel as if they were really clean. I even had a ritual of how I removed the dishes from the dishwasher to put them away. I'd put a glass this way, that way, you know—every which way.

Any kinds of switches or buttons could be trouble, even in the car. I'd turn the lights on, turn them off, turn them on, turn them off, turn them on, turn them off. Sometimes I'd put the window down, roll it up, put it down again. It's the strangest thing. You know you turned the lights off and you know they are off. But then you turn them on. I don't know why you turn them on in order to prove they were off, but that becomes a habit too.

During the last few years just before I started the program, my entire day except for sleep was preoccupied with my symptoms. I wasn't going anywhere because I was afraid to go places. Just getting out of the house was a chore. I did have a part-time job, and thank God, I did get there most of the time. Getting out of the apartment for a while gave me some relief.

I had blisters on my hands from washing so much but kept right on washing. My husband would open up those blisters for me and I kept right on. I was crying all the time, tired all the time, and ritualizing all the time. Some days I slept the whole day away. I didn't want to get out of bed.

Then I made an appointment at the clinic. I started to cry just filling out the first couple of questions on the questionnaire, because I knew I was in the right place. I just felt so relieved that someone actually knew what I was going through. I had not wanted to go on living, and now I thought maybe there was a chance.

I was very scared when my therapist first described the program, because he told me I would have to dirty my hands and arms and I wouldn't be able to wash. I didn't know if I'd be able to do it or not. He said he would not make me do anything he wouldn't do. I told him I would do anything to get better. He said hand washing was one of the easiest things to get rid of in behavior therapy, so I felt fortunate there. But in my mind I didn't see how it was going to work. A couple of nights before therapy began, I became very depressed. I just thought, "I don't know how it's going to work. Am I going to be able to do it? And if it doesn't work, what is going to happen to me?"

At the same time I also felt safe, that it was going to work, whatever it was going to be. I remember telling my therapist that I would roll in shit if I had to in order to get well, because I couldn't go on anymore. I made up my mind that I was going to do anything he told me to do. I didn't care how anxious I got or what I was going to have to do. I must say that the therapy wasn't anything compared to what I suffered before I got to treatment. That was the real surprising part.

On the first day of the program the therapist told me I would not be able to wash. The only thing he let me do was brush my teeth. Well, that was a little difficult to handle, especially going to the bathroom and not being able to wash afterward.

I decided to give the program my very best effort. Before, if I was lying in bed reading a book at night and felt dirty, I would probably have thrown the book away. Now I just made up my mind that I was going to stop that kind of behavior. I decided I wasn't going to let something like that bother me, and that's all there was to it.

Then the therapist started putting ink on my hands. He inked me in red and black all over. He wanted me to know by looking at my hands that they were dirty. He also wanted the ink to be able to rub off a little on things I touched. When my hands sweated, some of the ink transferred onto things I was touching. I can remember sitting in a chair watching TV. When I took my hand off the arm, there were my fingerprints. The ink bothered me but not nearly as much as I thought it was going to.

As I said, I just made up my mind I wasn't going to let things bother me. I'd get up in the morning and put deodorant on my sweaty armpits. In the past I might have done that once, but then I would have thrown the deodorant away. My therapist would put my comb through a bar of soap and then make me use it. He would make me put trash in my bed, like Kleenex, gum wrappers, pieces of paper, stuff I had in my waste can. I'd dump it in and then jump into bed and sleep with it. After a while you forget it's there.

It still works for me today. Even now, if I feel something is dirty, like shoes, I will keep wearing them and wearing them, and after a bit I no longer think about them being dirty. After you continue to expose yourself to these things, you forget. You just forget. Exposure is the key to getting well.

When I was allowed to take my first shower in the program I was petrified. My therapist told me I had ten minutes to complete it. I thought, "I'll never finish in that time. He'll have to come in and drag me out, I know he will, 'cause I can't do it." I was used to taking an hour. A lot of OCD people wash even longer.

I was not allowed to ritualize in the shower. He turned the water on for me at the right temperature and told me exactly how to hold the soap, how to wash, what to wash, and how to rinse. I jumped in the shower and only ritualized a little bit. It wasn't as bad as I thought. After eight minutes he knocked on the door to let me know I only had two minutes left. When I turned the water off and told him I was finished, he instructed me to take the bar of soap off the floor of the shower and put it outside on the sink. Then, of course, my hand was a mess.

He then said to take my towel and wipe my hand, then dry the rest of my body with the towel. Well, I did it, but that suggestion really scared me because I had lots of rituals around drying off. I'd use one towel for my face, another for my body, and I'd use one side of the towel for this, and another side of the towel for that. I wasn't allowed to do that during the program, of course. In that first attempt I was able to shower, dry off, and get dressed within ten minutes. I couldn't believe it! I felt really good. I even forgot about the soap on my hands.

The next time I showered he made me wash my hair. I hadn't washed my hair in years because it would take me too long. I used to go to the beauty shop instead. Now I wash my hair every day when I shower. I was petrified that first time: I was trying to shampoo my hair and get out of the shower within ten minutes, and I did it. It really made me feel good because I thought of all the rituals I used to do while taking a shower and now I didn't have to do them.

The program is about becoming knowledgeable. I left it with tools I can use to control my symptoms. For instance, if I am washing my hands and say to myself that I'm not doing it right, a voice in my head will say, "You want to do it again." I'll say to myself, "No, I am going to purposefully do it wrong. I'm doing it all wrong; it's all wrong, and I don't care." I just shut off those negative thoughts. If I am making the bed, sometimes I will find myself smoothing and smoothing. I'll purposefully wrinkle up the covers, then walk away. This way I am able to do these tasks normally without having to go through any of that compulsive stuff.

If I feel something—like a pocketbook—is dirty, and if I keep using it and using it and try to put it out of my mind, a week or so later I might say, "Well, I thought this was dirty; I wonder why I thought this was dirty?" If you avoid contact with that item, you'll build more of a compulsion around it.

It's easier for me to understand my problem now. When I start doing some little things like before, I no longer think I'm going crazy. I say, "You're an obsessive-compulsive, Shirley. That's why you're doing it. Now stop it!" It's just so much easier now. When you don't understand the problem it feels so overwhelming.

When I finished the program I felt wonderful! In fact, one day shortly after I finished therapy I called my therapist and started to cry. I said, "I can't believe I am this well," and I really cried with joy. You don't know what a thrill it is walking into a bathroom and washing your hands like so-called normal people do, or getting up in the morning, emptying the trash, and doing things you think normal people do without going through all those horrible rituals. I was able to get ready for work almost an hour earlier than before the program because I didn't go through all those rituals with washing my hands and combing my hair. At that time I would say I was really 99 percent better.

I think the secret to my recovery was wanting to get well. I had to get well. I didn't want to continue to live that way, and I don't think I would have. My whole life was consumed with the symptoms. I couldn't enjoy anything or anyone. Just watching TV, my mind would start wandering half of the time, wondering how I was going to get through this or that. I was tired all the time, just completely overwhelmed by everything. I wouldn't even be here without the program. I know that. I'd either be dead or locked away. I'm very grateful neither happened to me.

After the program I remember walking down the street and feeling very light all of a sudden. I thought I was going to fly for a moment, and I thought, "Why do I feel so light?" Then it dawned on me that I wasn't dragging that horrible, compulsive stuff with me anymore. That terrible weight wasn't on my shoulders anymore. That's why I was so light! I felt like a feather flying down the street, and it seemed so weird to me that I didn't have that terrible feeling around me anymore.

Today, after three years, I'd say I'm still 95 percent better. I'm working a lot now. I have two jobs. I think the key to my staying well is being busy. If I have a day off sometimes and don't have too much planned, I can tell the biggest difference. I don't become involved in a lot of ritualizing, but I can see that if I sit around too long I could get myself into a lot of problems again by not having my mind occupied. Keeping busy is very, very good.

I think talking about it is also good. It's good to confide in somebody you can trust. Even if the person doesn't understand, at least you can trust him or her with your problem. That is something I didn't do before, and I think I could have gotten help a lot sooner if I had. Of course I didn't know my problem had a name at first. Now it is out, you know it has a name, and you know there is help and you are not a freak.

I feel that behavior therapy is the only way to go. I was on a lot of drugs. They certainly didn't help with the obsessive-compulsive bit. They helped a little with the anxiety, but the facing of those fears, that's the key. The compulsions are a habit we build and build on. My therapist said it takes about three weeks to break your habits and to go through all these horrible things you thought you could never go through.

It was almost like a miracle to me. Finding the right help is the hardest part. I am very angry at the doctors for not being aware of behavior therapy for OCD. Giving us one pill after the other is no answer.

You really have to want to get well and stop those crazy things that take over your life. There is more to life than our crazy rituals. I used to sit and think about the fact that other people are concerned with life and death, their children and school. And what in the hell am I thinking about? How I am going to get up and go over there and wash my hands and try to get back here to the couch within two hours. Is that living? It's not living; it's hardly even existing. To get well you really have to want to get well and trust the program.

❦ *Joel*

Joel is a thirty-two-year-old father who began to experience severe obsessions about three years ago. For the next two years he was plagued with horrible thoughts and urges of harming members of his family. Although he reached out for professional help immediately, neither the therapy nor the medications he tried brought any relief to his suffering.

Then, one year ago, Joel began to learn the self-help techniques of cognitive-behavioral therapy. Here he explains how his problem started, the ways in which the symptoms have controlled his life, and finally how he is currently using his self-help skills to control his symptoms:

I got married at twenty-seven, and we had our daughter that next year. I became very protective of her. I was scared to death that she would die of crib death or get hurt. I wasn't confident in my ability to take care of her.

One night I was home alone, baby-sitting her. I was watching a police show while my daughter was sleeping in her crib. During a commercial I went in to check on her as I usually do, three or four times a night. All of a sudden I had this thought that I could kill her, that I might strangle her with a cord or stab her with a knife. My immediate reaction was "I could never hurt my daughter." Yet, I couldn't banish the negative thought from my head. I felt dizzy, my heart was racing, my legs became weak, and I started to shake. I was sweating severely and I immediately had diarrhea.

I went into the bathroom and stood there for a minute, trying to figure out what was going on. I again told myself that I'd never hurt my daughter. I went back in to check on her, placing my hand on her back to make sure she was still breathing. Yet, I still couldn't shake the thought. When I tried to go to sleep that night I kept getting the same thought: "You could kill your daughter. Go ahead and kill your daughter," over and over and over. I guess if I had known about OCD at that time, I wouldn't have become so frightened about my thoughts.

For the next two weeks that's all I thought about. I was bedridden in the mornings for probably three or four days. I got very depressed, and I just couldn't force myself out of the bed. I finally returned to work, but I continued to dwell on the thought that I could kill my daughter and on thoughts that God was telling me to do this. All kinds of frightening notions came to my mind, like the thought that she was a devil. I avoided knives, and I avoided being alone at home with her. After about two weeks of this horrible mental anguish I had lost about twenty pounds.

I never said anything to anyone. Finally, I got to the point where I had to tell someone, so I told my wife. After I explained to her what was taking place and got it off my chest, I felt fine for three or four days. Then, slowly but surely, the thoughts returned: "You could kill your daughter." Then my next thought would be, "I'd never hurt my daughter." That became my seemingly endless ritual, to repeat, "I'll never hurt my daughter."

My symptoms got worse and worse as time went on. I continued to work, but I was also crying throughout the day and I felt guilty about thinking such terrible thoughts about my daughter. During this time there was a story in our paper about a woman who killed both of her kids. When I heard that news, it stunned me. I can remember that. I thought, "How could a person do that to her kids? What drives a person to do that?" For a couple of days I dwelled on it, and then it went away. One night a few weeks later all of a sudden it just popped into my head that I could go crazy like this woman. Then I became scared to death that I would go crazy and hurt someone.

Fortunately I continued to make myself stay home alone with my daughter because, even back when I first began having these terrible urges and thoughts, I knew that I shouldn't start avoiding. If I convinced myself that I wasn't capable of baby-sitting my daughter, I might have lost my courage to do much of anything.

I love my daughter more than anything else in the world, and I would protect her more than anything, just like anyone else who has a child. Imagine all of a sudden having an urge to kill the one thing you love the most, and to have the physical reaction of a full-fledged panic attack at the same time. I was terrified by it! I don't know what scared me more: the thoughts or the panic attacks. The panic attacks would come and go, but the urge to kill myself or kill my child sometimes became constant, while I was working or playing.

When my wife asked me to watch the baby while she went out to the supermarket, I would immediately get this flash of fear: "This is going to be it; this is where I am going to lose control and kill my daughter." At other times, such as if I were on the second floor of a mall with my family, looking down to the bottom floor, all of a sudden I'd have this thought: "Oh, I could just chuck her over this railing and splat her on the ground." These thoughts would be terribly frightening and would badger me.

Sometimes when I got a little tired or a little bored, these horrible thoughts would be the first thing that popped into my mind. Say that I was sitting down at the supper table talking to my wife and daughter. If there was a little lull in the conversation, all of a sudden I'd just have the thought, "Well, you could reach over and kill her." Then I would become anxious and sweaty. I couldn't wait to go to bed at night just because when I slept I didn't think about it.

I became so aware of every thought I had that my fears just skipped from one idea to another. My predominant and most painful thought was killing my daughter, but then it would spread out into killing myself or killing my wife. I became frightened of seeing guns. If I saw a policeman walking down the street, the first thing I would look at was his gun. All of a sudden I would think, "Oh, I could pull that gun out and shoot myself."

Finally I found out about the OCD program at the Center for the Treatment and Study of Anxiety. That was about two years after my first symptoms began. I can remember my first session vividly. I spent the majority of the time crying because I was pretty depressed and I didn't know where to turn. The therapist reassured me that I wasn't going crazy and that a cognitive-behavioral program could help me.

In our first session, the therapist told me I would never kill my daughter. I was constantly looking for that kind of certainty. She also told me that behavioral treatment can help and that lots of people get good results from it, even though some people don't. I walked out of that office feeling as if I was cured and would never have problems again. It was because someone had given me answers. The most important answer I can remember was that other people also have this problem.

I also did my first exposure practice. The therapist asked me to describe into a tape recorder the details of how I would kill my daughter. Well, I got about one sentence out and I couldn't go any further. I couldn't even imagine saying out loud that I would kill my daughter. I believed that if I said it out loud, all of a sudden I wouldn't have control over my thoughts. It was essential for me to believe I was in control. If I could just say, "Well, that thought doesn't mean anything to me," then I wouldn't have this problem. However, when I had those thoughts, I believed I couldn't control them, and they would become real. So I got about one sentence out and couldn't go any further.

I did just a little better with the tape recording in our second session, three or four days later. I was able to say, "I'll come home, I'll lose control, and I'll kill my daughter."

For homework after that second session the therapist asked me to write a page on exactly how I would kill her. This assignment was hard because I never let myself say or attempt to know *how* I was going to kill my daughter. I would just have that urge and then begin to say, "I'll never do it," and that would be it. But it began to take me longer and longer to convince myself that I'd never hurt my daughter.

So in the exposure program I began to create the specific situations in which I could kill my daughter. By the third session I was able to write a one-page story about it. Then the therapist asked me to write a three-page story for homework over the weekend. I dreaded writing it, and when I did finish it, I was worn out. But it made me think about it, and honestly, after about forty-five minutes of writing, I felt better. I still had the fear, but I didn't feel compelled to say over and over to myself, "I'll never hurt my daughter, I'll never hurt my daughter." I didn't have my typical need to ritualize. Eventually I got up to writing about five pages.

My stories tended to run in the same general direction: I would come home from work dazed and confused, get out of the car, enter the house, and just lose control. I would stab my daughter and stab my wife. I included my wife in the stories because I was scared I would hurt other people as well as my daughter.

I was also afraid I would kill myself. So in some stories I would come home, stab my daughter, and my wife would be screaming and hollering. Then I would stab her. My daughter would say, "Daddy, don't do that." My wife would scream, "Don't hurt her, don't hurt her." And I would scream, "I have to, this is what I've got to do." Then, at the end of the story I would stab myself but would live. The cops would come and drag me out of the house. I'd still be alive to face how I had let my parents and family down. Everyone would think I was a scumbag. I'd spend the rest of my life in prison, but I wouldn't be crazy. I would have the full guilt of what I did and all I would want to do was die, but there was no way I could.

I also had a fear that God was telling me to kill my daughter. In this kind of treatment, you need to face your fears as directly as possible. So the therapist created a tape with someone else's voice. It was one of those sixty-second loop tapes that played again and again. On the tape a man's voice said, "Go ahead, kill your daughter. I am God." I practiced listening to it each night while my wife was home.

Then one night my wife was out shopping and I was baby-sitting. I forced myself to listen to the tape for an hour, even though I was terribly uncomfortable. Afterward, I never had that fear again, the fear that God is going to tell me to kill my daughter. I still have the memory of those thoughts, but I no longer feel anxious about them.

I have progressed to a point where I feel that my practice has probably made me 80 percent better. But I still have some bad times. I know that if I could just get to the point of saying that the thoughts don't matter anymore, then I'd really be done with this problem. I want to get to the point where I believe that the thoughts and the actions have nothing to do with each other. I can do that most of the time now but not all of the time.

Before I did the self-help program I couldn't face my fears at all. I figured that one day this would just wear me down. I'm more confident now. I can face my fears in such a way that they just don't surface as much anymore. Quite a bit of the time I don't have any fears at all. I occasionally have the fears of hurting my daughter, my wife, or myself. Every now and then I have a hard bout with it. But when that happens I just have to face them. Sometimes I can and sometimes I can't. The program made me realize that when I face the fearful situation and make the negative thoughts come, the urge will disappear.

If I start to have trouble with a fear again, it generally just takes me one hour of facing it to regain control. If I really force myself to have the thoughts, then after about thirty minutes I get bored with them. I keep the thoughts coming for the second half hour, even though they don't bother me as much anymore. So as long as I force myself to do that exposure for an hour or to make sure I write that extra thirty minutes in my homework practice, I'll turn the corner and can move on with my life and when I'm done practicing I'm tired!

A couple of months ago my wife took a trip by herself, leaving me with my daughter. The first day was hard. When I got in the car that morning my initial thought was, "Well, I could slam the car into a pole." That thought really scared me so I tried to stay very busy all day long to keep myself occupied. The second day was a little better. I got my thoughts more in order, and I figured I would start facing my fears directly. So when we got up in the morning, instead of running out to see somebody or do something, we stayed and played in the living room for a couple of hours. I discovered that when I am home with my daughter for an extended period the urges aren't so bad. It's the same lesson: When you face your fears directly, after about an hour the urge begins to subside.

Before I had behavior therapy it just seemed that I was getting worse and worse and worse. Now I get up in the morning and know immediately whether it's going to be a good day or a bad day. I just say to myself, "Well, if it's going to be a bad day, then tomorrow will be a good day." I also know that if I do my practice correctly, the bad day will not be as bad.

❦ Annette

Annette began to experience OCD symptoms as a child. For over two decades she continuously worried about death and chronic illnesses—cancer, brain tumors, leukemia, multiple sclerosis—and desperately sought reassurances from any authority in attempts to relieve her fears. At age thirty-two she began the three-week program. Six years later, this is her story:

The first symptoms I can remember were at about age seven. We had just moved to a new house. I started developing an irrational fear that something horrible was going to happen to my teeth. I had always hated going to the dentist; I had cavities from the time I was four years old. I know now that the worst thing that could have happened is that all of my teeth would have fallen out. Yet I had a real panic of something vague and horrible occurring. After about a year or so that fear seemed to fade away.

I remember a couple of years later finding my uncle's pediatric-medicine books and looking at all those horrible diseases kids could develop. I'd ask my uncle to promise I was not going to have those illnesses. These worries lasted for years. I would become panicky about my thoughts and seek out my uncle. He would reassure me, and that would help for a short while, but then the worries would come back.

My parents always tried to protect me from death and pain.

I think that had an adverse effect on me because I never learned how to cope with anything unpleasant. When I was in elementary school one of my friends got leukemia. I really believed she was going to be OK, that they were going to save her. But she kept getting sicker and sicker, and finally she died. I was shocked. In a sense it was like growing up: There aren't any guarantees, and medicine can't always save you. That event had a lasting effect on me.

In my teenage years I began to fear getting cancer. I would talk to people about it and watch their reaction. If they said, "Yes, I'm afraid too," then my anxiety would go up. I would then have to go back and talk to them, to seek their reassurance that everything was going to be OK. I wanted them to give me guarantees that I wasn't going to die of cancer, that nothing bad was going to happen to me.

I soon focused on leukemia, MS, and brain tumors because I had known people who had those problems. I worried that such illnesses were contagious. The doctors would reassure me that they weren't, but nobody was quite sure how people developed them. "Well," I thought, "if you don't know how people get them then you can't be a hundred percent certain they're not contagious."

These basic fears remained throughout my life. When I read an article a few years ago about the theory associating cancer and stress, I thought I was going to lose my mind. I felt I was going to cause myself to have cancer because of the stress of worrying about cancer!

I continuously asked people such as nurses, my uncle, my dad, about these illnesses. "What do you think about this mole on my arm? Does it look serious? Do you promise me it's not cancer?" After a while I began to hate seeing my uncle because I would have to work so hard at not asking him questions. At the same time, while being with him I felt compelled to think of all the things that were wrong with me so I could ask him if I was going to be OK. It was always a fight: Do I ask him these things or do I shut up about them? This conflict was too much for me. It was just easier not to see him at all.

There was always another question. I would think to myself, "What if one of these diseases is in this paint?" "What if this cleanser I'm using has germs in it?" There was always another mole or freckle, an ache or a pain. For instance, I knew there was a connection between bruising and leukemia because it was a blood disorder. When I was anxious I would squeeze my thumb again and again to the point where it caused a little bruise. Then I'd call the doctor and say, "I've touched my thumb and it's bruising." I would develop concerns like that endlessly and seek assurance.

I would never say the word *cancer* or the word *leukemia*. I wouldn't even spell those words because it was a bad omen. It would be bad luck.

I had only a couple of rituals that magically made me feel safe. If I touched someone who was contaminated with cancer, then I would need to touch a "strong" person, like my uncle or my father, in order to feel somehow "protected." Sometimes washing helped, but I would not just wash my hands. In order to feel safe, I would have to wash whatever clothes I was wearing before I washed myself. Whatever I touched had to be washed.

Nuclear power became an issue. And radiation. And the chemicals that cause different kinds of cancers. I used to live near a nuclear-power plant. I would call their 800 number to find out how many rads were being emitted each day and what direction the wind was blowing to decide whether it was OK to be outside. If I were ever driving close by the power plant I would roll up the windows as though somehow that would help protect me.

I read volumes of information about all of these fears. The part I couldn't figure out was how much exposure to these chemicals or germs it would take to cause a problem. That was the missing link for me. I couldn't get balanced, I couldn't get perspective. If I had to have an X ray, I nearly lost my mind. I wouldn't have tooth X rays. I would make up anything, like telling them I thought I was pregnant, so I wouldn't have to explain why I didn't want an X ray. It wouldn't matter how many times I read the pamphlets saying this is low-level radioactivity. I was convinced it was going to get me and that I could trust no one to tell me the truth.

I love fishing, but I read articles about kinds of fish cancer they had discovered in the Great Lakes. So when I caught a fish I would look it over very carefully. If it had any mark on it then I would almost lose my mind. "How am I going to get this fish off my hook? How am I ever going to touch this hook again?" So I would cut the whole line. Lures are expensive. They cost three, four, sometimes five dollars. I lost a lot of lures! I simply couldn't touch them again. I remember quizzing a game warden at a lake about these marks on the fish. He explained them to me, but I wasn't satisfied. I got very good at asking the same question in a number of different ways in an attempt to bring down my anxiety. But I could never get it down. No answer was ever quite enough, no matter how many questions I asked.

I just knew that I was going to catch this illness. It was going to get me. It was going to destroy me. My death would be slow and painful and completely horrible. I would die in complete panic. I wouldn't be able to get away, and I wouldn't be able to stop it. Once I got cancer there would never be any rest. It would be a horror show for months.

The first day I started the treatment program I had an interview with my therapist and the director of the treatment program. The director asked me what I was afraid of. I said, "Leukemia," and she said, "We may have to get some leukemia blood." At that moment my knees just went out from under me. I felt the blood go out of my head. I put my foot against the wall to hold myself up, and I remember thinking, "I can't do this, I can't possibly do this."

All I could think about was having to touch that blood. I

looked at my therapist, and it was obvious he was in agreement with the director. It was like all of a sudden finding out I was in an enemy camp. I knew what exposure therapy was, but I didn't think it was going to be that bad. I thought perhaps I would use binoculars to look into a leukemia patient's room to start with, then slowly I would have to stand outside of the room and wave. Maybe I would open the window and close it very quickly, but I would never touch blood! I called up my best friend later that day and said, "Be at the airport, I'm coming to visit." She told me I couldn't leave. I explained what the treatment program involved, but she insisted I had to stay. She just kept talking to me until I agreed.

We worked with imagery during the program. For instance, regarding leukemia, I made an extended tape about my feared consequences. The imageries made me very frightened, but we did them day after day. Pretty soon, hearing the same story six or seven times, listening both in the morning and the afternoon, they became less scary.

At the same time I was working on my fear of bone marrow. My therapist made me go to the butcher's, buy some bone marrow, then drive around with it in the car, touching it and putting it on my clothes and my face. I had to spray it with Lysol and smell it and then touch it. I wasn't allowed to wash my hands for days. We'd even go out to eat without washing my hands first. I felt like a totally deranged person. I felt so dirty.

Then I slept with the bone marrow under my pillow. I drove around Philadelphia with dirty hands, walked around dirty people, and carried this paper bag with bone marrow in it everywhere I went. After three or four days the bone marrow didn't bother me much because I knew the practice with leukemia blood was coming up next. It was like working with bone marrow was being in nursery school.

The first day we practiced with blood, my therapist put the vial on the arm of the chair next to me. The next day he placed the vial on the chair with the top off. The day after that, I had to touch the blood. Then I put it on my hands and on my face. My therapist put it on himself as well. I felt somehow that if he could do it, then it wasn't so bad.

In a later session we put the blood in a spray bottle and sprayed it all over my house. I ate sandwiches after spraying the blood on my hands.

The first time I touched the blood I cried because I knew I was dying. I knew I had lost. I felt the fight was over, and I was going to die. I'd just done the worst thing I could possibly do. In a way that helped me get through it. There was no point in fighting anymore, so I could surrender. The way I was living I was already dead. I was scared all the time, and people thought I was crazy. I obsessed over things that no one else even bothered about. That's no way to live. It was as though the world was synchronized and I was not.

After one week I was not afraid of the blood anymore. I wasn't sure if I could die from it, but I just wasn't as bothered. One reason is that I trusted my therapist. Also I just couldn't live anymore with that intense level of anxiety. Third, I began to learn ways to manage my anxiety. Once I found out there were ways other than my rituals to handle my anxiety, then I could start believing I was normal. It wasn't that I stopped having the thoughts, because I would still think, "What if that blood really makes me have leukemia?" But then I would say, "So what. There's nothing I can do about it now. It's done. If anything is going to happen, I don't have control of it anymore."

I began to think more logically. "People have blood on them often. People come into the emergency room, people ride in ambulances. They don't panic. I can relax, it will be okay." When I kept thinking this way then I didn't become as anxious. I started to believe what the rest of the world believes.

I had a strong urge to wash during this time of touching the blood. I managed it by just clenching my fist and trying to keep busy. I went to the movies and got on buses and tried to be around people. I walked and walked and walked. On one bus there was a drunk who kept falling down. Everyone was laughing at him, and he was about to fall off the seat. I thought, "He's dirty and who knows what he's got?" But I made myself go over and sit him up. Afterward I was glad I didn't panic. The more I did things like that, the less I panicked. The less I panicked, the stronger I got.

At first, I felt my worst anxiety when I touched the blood. Yet soon, the anxiety would come up only until the point when I touched the blood. I learned that all I had to do was take the action and then I wouldn't feel bad. That was my incentive. I thought, "If you want to get rid of this anxiety, then just do it." And then I would, and my anxiety would start to dissipate. In the past when I would do some of these things by mistake, through error, my anxiety would skyrocket for days. Performing an action *deliberately* made the anxiety go away.

After working on my fear of blood, we traveled to the nuclear-power plant for a picnic. That was very frightening to me, but not only because the power plant had low-level radioactivity. My elementary-school friend, who died of leukemia, had lived nearby. I was convinced she had gotten leukemia from the nuclear-power plant.

We picnicked in the snow that day by the plant. Both of us ate some of the snow because, you know, snow carries radioactivity down through the air. We opened up the trunk, got the blood out, and had the blood there in the snow. The blood was always around us. Even if we weren't doing anything with it, it had to be there.

Then we went into the power plant. My therapist kept asking them to give us a tour, but their tour guide wasn't available. Of course my thought was that the person doing the tours was not available because there was some kind of nuclear accident going on. Now, I thought, both the therapist and I were exposed to everything, so we were both going to die. At least I wasn't going to be alone!

At the end of the program, my therapist traveled with me to my home, carrying his little vial of blood with him. We put the blood in the plant sprayer and mixed it with water. Then we sprayed it all over the house. He opened the cupboards and put it all over my plates and dishes and silverware; he dumped some in the humidifier. It was disgusting! He sprayed the coffeepot and then we drank coffee. As long as I didn't do rituals I was okay.

When I finished the program I felt so empowered. I felt I was doing well. I wasn't afraid of these things anymore. I occasionally had thoughts that my therapist was wrong, but they didn't have strong impact. I figured if he was wrong then so was half the world and we're all in trouble. So I was at least more synchronized with everybody else and I was really proud of myself that I had done the program. I called up friends at home and said, "Guess what I did." They would say things like, "God, I don't have the courage that you have. I could never have done that."

It's been six years since my program. I don't think about cancer being contagious. If it is, it is, and if it isn't, it isn't. It doesn't really matter. I don't have any fears about leukemia. I can go work with leukemia patients. I think I have a normal precaution about radioactivity. I don't like X rays, but you have to have them. I have my teeth X-rayed as needed. I didn't have X rays when I was pregnant. I'm probably more sensitive to the radiation than the average person who has never thought about it, but it does not control me. I say, "OK, is this X ray necessary? If it is, I let them do it. And if it isn't, I don't let them do it." I would say I'm 90 percent improved.

I'd like to say one thing to others with OCD. They don't have to live like that. Probably there will always be a tendency to have symptoms, but to be overpowered by them is unnecessary. If they can just believe enough in the program and then decide to just *do it*, just *do* the actions, then the problem will become manageable. It can be manageable forever once you have the tools to get it under control. It may come back, but not ever like it was. I don't believe that it will ever again consume me, even though I recognize that I will always have a tendency to worry. But I now know what I need to do. You're not going to make it unless you just *do it*.

❧ Kate

Like Annette, Kate first experienced symptoms of obsessive worries at an early age—thirteen years old. Her fears dominated her life for fifteen years and included washing, checking, and repeating rituals as well as obsessions about hurting herself and her family. Six months after she participated in the program, she spoke about her recovery:

I'm twenty-nine years old, I'm married, and I have a baby. My obsessive-compulsive problem has made everything a real struggle. It's gotten in the way of my personal relationships and in the way of my career. I have spent a great deal of time and energy warding off danger. One of the main reasons I sought help was because of the fears I had about my baby.

I feel proud because I have been successful in my career, despite my handicap. But it's only been through this program and by talking to other people about my problem that I've been able to let go of some of the shame I've always felt about it. I am really very happy with the results of the treatment. Even though I still have a lot to do, it's unbelievable. I never thought that anything would help me. I've tried so many things and nothing worked.

My symptoms began when I was thirteen, but I have a feeling it was there lying dormant much earlier than that. When I was a child I used to be very superstitious. If I wore a certain dress one day and had something bad happen that day, I would be afraid to wear that dress again. It would just hang in my closet. Looking back I think that was an OC symptom.

In high school any situation that could be remotely connected with danger was off-limits for me. For example, I was afraid to walk in the woods because I associated nature with those movies where people go camping and some guy comes and kills them with a chain saw. Whenever I was in a pretty place in nature, that's what I would think about: some mad killer lurking about. When I saw knives I didn't think of chopping vegetables, I thought of being stabbed. At some point those thoughts evolved into being afraid I would stab someone with a knife. I even became afraid of drills because I had seen a movie where someone got drilled to death. Rationally, I knew that none of these things would happen, but the thoughts still scared me.

I worried that all of a sudden I would do something that would harm me. When I went to amusement parks with my friends, I couldn't go on the rides. Once in college I went to Disneyland with friends and rode on the Matterhorn. It's a roller coaster ride that goes through a pretend mountain made of plaster of paris. You travel through tunnels. I was afraid I would have the sudden impulse to stand up, that I wouldn't have the impulse control necessary to stay in my seat, and I'd be killed.

My obsessive fears made me a very dependent person, and it was humiliating. I had fears that some crazy person who escaped from an insane asylum would break into our house and kill me. Or a spy would hide out in my house, hold me hostage, and then kill me. Every time an airplane flew over I was afraid that it might be carrying an atomic bomb. If I had a little itch on my leg I thought I had blood poisoning. I lived in constant terror that all of a sudden I would have an aneurysm. It was like being in a war, living in a concentration camp where you don't know if you are going to be killed in the next second.

I spent a year away in college, but I just floundered there and eventually returned home. I remember I had acne that year, so the doctor prescribed tetracycline. I had to open the capsules and mix them in my orange juice because I was afraid to take the capsule whole. I worried that someone might have put poisonous drugs in it. So once I put it in the orange juice and stirred it up, I wouldn't drink all of the orange juice. I figured if there was some poison in there and I didn't drink it all, I might survive. I just accepted these kinds of rituals as part of my life. I would avoid many foods. I would never buy food off the street from vendors. I only bought fresh foods and cooked them myself. I didn't buy candy bars or packaged foods that someone might be able to put drugs in. It was terribly embarrassing, and I tried to hide it.

Despite these problems, I managed to hold down a good job, to get married, and have a child. Things got much worse when I became pregnant. I was so scared of something happening to the fetus that I was afraid to eat anything. When you are pregnant, people are continually telling you what foods are bad for you. That really got to me. I was afraid to eat meat, I was afraid to eat chicken because of the new incidents of salmonella. I was even afraid to eat eggs. I knew rationally that you can simply cook the foods and get rid of the salmonella, but I was afraid, for instance, that if I touched the chicken and then touched something else, I would contaminate it.

Every meal was fraught with anxiety. Every time I went shopping I had to examine everything I bought because it wasn't just me I was protecting anymore, it was the baby. It would take my husband and me a long time to grocery shop, and then I would throw things away once we got home. I would take out a can of tomatoes, and if there was a tiny little dent in it I would throw it away because I was afraid somehow it would be tainted with botulism.

At the time my baby was born I still had the fear of food poisoning from botulism and salmonella. But the strongest fear was losing control and hurting my child. I saw a show on postpartum psychoses on TV in which they talked about women who became psychotic after their baby was born and then killed their child. So I started to be afraid that I too would become psychotic and kill my baby.

I developed all kinds of rituals around my baby. I had to wash my hands four or five times before I could pick him up. When I changed his diaper, I'd put it on and then it wouldn't feel right. I'd have to pick up his legs and move the diaper a little bit, and then move it a little more. I'd tape it and then I'd untape it and retape it until it felt okay.

The hardest part was putting him to bed at night. I would put him down, then I'd have to pick him up again sometimes and put him down again and pick him up and put him down. I'd cover him and then I'd have to pull the blanket back and cover him again. I couldn't go back in to look at him once I got him in the bed and left the room. I would make my husband go and check. I knew if I went into the room I'd start my rituals again. It would take me five minutes each time before I could get back out of the room. So once I was able to get out of the room I wouldn't want to go back in.

After I had the baby I realized that things were getting worse. My husband was having problems as well. I was very demanding of him. He was working full-time during the day, and then I didn't want him to leave the house at night because I was afraid to be alone with the baby. It was causing a lot of trouble. So we were seeing a counselor together. I talked to her about my problem and she told me about the treatment program. I was very scared before I came to the clinic. It was a big deal for me to address this problem specifically, because I always skirted around it.

When the program was described to me it definitely made sense. I thought it actually might work for certain things. Yet, there were things I thought would be too hard to do. I remember having exposure explained to me, that I would have to stop doing my rituals. I said, "Sure," but inside I thought, "No way." The therapist said we might go to some drug-infested neighborhood and I would eat something off the ground. That part of the program sounded terrifying to me.

As it turned out, I was able to do everything. I never actually went to that drug-infested neighborhood and ate something off the ground, but I did comparable things. There was a guy selling pretzels on the side of the highway. He was wearing fatigues, and he looked like a real sleaze-ball. He had milk crates covered with pretzels. I bought one and ate the whole thing. That was as good as eating something off the ground in a drug-infested neighborhood. It was terrifying to me, but nothing happened.

I think I have improved 75 percent. My OC problem is still there, and I know it's always going to be there, but I also know that I can do something about it now. I don't have to keep making my world smaller and smaller the way I used to. Before the program, I didn't think there was any hope for me. I thought there was nothing I could do to make myself feel better. My attitude has completely changed after the program. I don't feel like a victim to my illness anymore. Now I know I have control.

The fears I was having about hurting my son are virtually gone. I have freedom with my baby that I didn't have before. At those rare times when I have thoughts of harming him, I know they're just thoughts and my fear about those thoughts is much less. I can give him a bath. I can go in and check on him at night. I touch his face and I don't feel compelled to touch it again. I was alone with him for two weeks while my husband was away. Before, I felt as if I was a basket case, as if I could barely take care of him. Now I feel I can really be his mother and that change is wonderful.

When I have momentary obsessive thoughts or urges, they don't really frighten me anymore. I use those moments as opportunities to practice my skills. Like tonight, when I thought about talking to my therapist, I began to review my fears. Then I glanced at a knife on the counter in my kitchen, and all of a sudden I felt afraid. So I picked up the knife and held it against my chest as an exposure practice. That took away the threat.

I also know that this disorder, at least in my case, seems to be cyclical. I think there will be periods of time when I will have more anxiety than others, but I don't think it's going to control my life again.

One thing I learned is that it's harder anticipating doing the exposure practice than it is to actually do it. The practice is hard, of course, but it always works. The fear always goes down after a certain amount of time. As I continued in the program I came to believe that. There were times when my therapist and I were on the roof during a practice session. I would say, "I can't stand this, I can't stand this. I'm going to go back inside." He would continue to encourage me, saying, "Just stay out here. If you can stay here longer, it's going to go down." And it did. The fear always went down. Instead of being ashamed of having this problem I'm trying really hard to be proud of overcoming it.

My advice to anyone with OCD is to get help. Follow the program or use a doctor who does exposure practice. It's the only way. I also feel that it's important to do some kind of stress-management together with the exposures. I do relaxation exercises every day now. In my opinion, anyone with an anxiety disorder should learn how to relax.

❦ *Gustina*

Gustina is a fifty-year-old divorced mother with two grown children. Twenty years ago she began to develop hand-washing rituals. Gradually over the years new rituals entered her daily life until she was practically consumed by them.

Gustina's story is a special one since she overcame most of her OCD symptoms using self-help skills and without any professional help:

I had severe depression back in '69. I was thirty at the time and having all kinds of marital and family problems. Previous to that I had no indications of OCD at all: none in my childhood, none in my high school years. But after becoming depressed I developed an urge to wash my hands. It was a fear of contamination that made me wash. I don't really know how I got it in my head that my hands were contaminated.

I didn't continually wash them throughout the day. At the beginning it only had to do with eating or cooking. I didn't mind getting my hands dirty, but if I had to eat or prepare food, they had to be washed and washed again. I wasn't thinking logically, because if I thought logically then I wouldn't have that fear.

I don't know that I could say it was fear of germs *per se,* but it was a fear of contamination. Now that I am looking back, I think I was afraid I was going to get into a depression if I didn't wash. I was so terrified of getting depressed again because that's a living hell and I would not have survived it a second time. I was also afraid of becoming anxious. I wanted to avoid the anxiety. Only it grew and grew and grew. If it had stayed at that low level I could have tolerated it, but it just grew.

From hand washing, it grew into wearing gloves while cleaning the house. Then I had to separate everything in the kitchen. I had my special section of the refrigerator for food. No one was allowed to touch it or use it. Then I would no longer empty wastebaskets because this would put dust in the air, which could contaminate the food. I got to the point where I would clean the house only on a certain night, because I had to prepare everything beforehand. I had to make sure the cupboards were closed properly in order to protect the food. I began to have problems with bathroom procedures. I had a rigid routine that would take me thirty-five minutes. I had to wash my hands repetitively after using the bathroom. I would wash them over the tub faucet because I could move more freely. The sink area was too small. I can remember bending over the tub for so long that my back and leg muscles would be killing me. After two or three minutes of bending you can start to feel it.

Every ritual had to be so precise and exact that I could not deviate at all. If I did, I had to go back and start again. The intensity was overwhelming. Sometimes I could do it without anxiety, but there were other times when the anxiety was so strong.

It got to the point that I just could not cook anymore. I stopped eating anything I touched. For years I didn't eat any finger foods like potato chips, pretzels, or sandwiches. I certainly learned that you could prepare food without actually ever even touching it, especially in these days of prepackaged foods. I could go on forever and never touch a morsel of food. I was even able to stop washing my hands while preparing food during this period, too, since they were no longer getting food-contaminated. But I did continue the ritual of washing my hands during other times, like after using the bathroom.

About six years ago I had another bout with depression. The OCD intensified during that time, and I grew more branches on this tree. For instance, I would never touch a cigarette. I always opened a pack of cigarettes and pulled the first one out with the foil that's in there, and the rest I could just jiggle out. I also would not touch my lips at all because my lips had to be clean to eat. I was protecting myself from anything that got into my blood as well as anything I ingested.

To clean my lips I would wet them and then wipe them with a paper towel before I ate anything. I had a complicated ritual associated with washing my lips: once in this direction, again in that direction, and so forth, until I was satisfied. I even cleaned my lips at work. I would hide from everyone in the back room where I stored paper towels.

If I knew I was not going to eat or smoke, then my lips didn't have to be cleansed. Yet, if I was going away for the day and I cleansed my lips before I left, I would not touch them at all during that whole day until maybe I was on the way home and I knew I had finished smoking or eating. Once I got home I knew I could cleanse them again. I would also blow on my lips if I had a sense that they were dirty and needed to be cleaned while I was out.

Here's what a typical day was like back when my symptoms were at their worst. The first thing I did in the morning was to cleanse my lips because I wanted to have a cigarette. Then I would have to go to the bathroom. I would spend twenty minutes to half an hour in the bathroom. It got to the point where I was timing myself because I would try to break that habit, at least by making it one minute shorter a day. If I made it in fifteen minutes, boy, that was great! But the next time some stress might cause me to stay in there for a half hour again, and all that effort was shot.

Then I would have my coffee. I would take a paper cup and turn it a certain number of times. I would drink my coffee only in a certain place in my kitchen: on my stool at the counter. There I would have a cup of coffee and a cigarette. I wouldn't smoke two cigarettes with a cup of coffee. In this ritual I was only allowed to smoke one. Once I was finished with the coffee, my lips were soiled again, so I would clean them. Then I would go into the bedroom to start getting ready for work. My lips would be soiled again, because I walked into another room where there was dust and dirt or whatever else was in the air. I was always cleaning my lips throughout the day, every time I'd change locations, even change rooms.

I would never smoke out of the same pack of cigarettes in different locations or on different days. I always took a fresh pack to work, or I bought them when I stopped to get my coffee. I would smoke them for the day, but at the end of the day I would not take that pack home. That pack was finished.

If I brought it with me out of the office it would be contaminated on the way home. So I would have cigarettes waiting for me at home. It cost a hell of a lot of money to be throwing out these half packs of cigarettes! At first I had a ritual of zipping the cigarettes into my purse in a certain way to seal them off. Then I got so tired of that ritual that I just said, "To hell with it, it's not worth it. I'll throw the cigarettes out." So that's how it happened.

Then a couple of years ago I saw a program on OCD on *20/20*. That's when I realized what my problem was. I found an OCD self-help support group in my town and joined it a year and a half ago.

The group had a very, very positive effect on me. Each òf us set our own goals, and we met every two weeks. Some weeks we had as few as three people attending and other weeks we had as many as ten, depending on who cared to make it. Being a take-charge type of person, I was the official secretary, taking the notes, calling the people, and doing whatever other chores needed to be done.

When I started the group I asked myself, "Do you want to get better?" I said, "Yes, I want to get better. Definitely. And the timing is right." First you have to decide to help yourself, then the group is great for moral support and encouragement. It's good for anyone who needs to know there are other OC's out there. It's good for advice and any kind of bonding you need while you go through this.

We all set goals, and we were all supposed to follow through on those goals. For instance, I decided I was going to give up one major problem area and five minor problem areas every two weeks. Sometimes I would do two or three big ones in those two weeks, but I started with the ones that were easier. I started with the cigarettes. I deliberately smoked the first one and the last two, which I wasn't able to do before. I used to take only two puffs out of a cigarette. So I also decided to smoke as much of a cigarette as I chose to.

Another example: I wouldn't touch my arm just above the elbow because it had become contaminated. That lasted for about three years. So on my list I decided I would begin to touch my elbow again. Not just for tomorrow but forever. To commit myself for one day is fine but that's only one day. I have the rest of my life. I have to do this forever. Once I decided to decontaminate it, then it was decontaminated. You can't try to stop your ritual just a little bit because it's like you're just a little bit pregnant. You either are or you aren't. Once I gave up a ritual I would never start it again. For me it had to be cold turkey. I couldn't just slow it down. It didn't work. I had to stop it, just stop it.

For instance, I had a problem with restaurants. If I ever looked at a restaurant during the day I couldn't return to it later that day. But on the way home from one of our meetings one night, I just stopped and decided to have a cup of coffee in a restaurant where I had eaten lunch. Once I decided to break that ritual, I never let it stop me again.

There were hundreds of patterns like that. I would never breathe through my mouth unless my lips were clean. You try that sometime and carry on a conversation! It's very difficult! I couldn't even wipe my mouth when I was eating because the napkin wasn't clean.

I would make my decisions very quickly about whether to stop a ritual. Often it would come at the point when I was about to begin that ritual. It would just hit me: "Well, I'm stopping this one right now." I wouldn't sit there and dwell on it, and I wouldn't methodically list out which ones I'd stop today and which tomorrow. I started with the smaller ones, knowing that eventually I was going to get to those big ones. I would tell myself, "I'll cross that bridge when I come to it. I'm working on these right now."

If one week I was working on a particular major ritual and five minor ones, I would only work on these. The rest of the rituals I continued because I could not stop them all at once.

That would have been mind-boggling—there were just too many. So I had to concentrate on a specific five or so. I started working on the least severe, because I had to start somewhere. It took me about a year to get to the more severe ones.

Several months ago I decided to join a therapy group led by a psychologist. In the self-help group some people aren't as motivated as others. You slack off a bit; people don't show up. But in the therapy group if you don't really want to get better, don't even bother coming. The self-help group was just perfect for working on all my other rituals. Once I was starting on the big ones I knew I had to get a little more professional help. This therapy group was limited to only four participants, and we met every two weeks.

It was in this group that I worked most actively on my eating troubles. Since this was the first ritual to come it seems to have been the toughest to get over, and it was the last to go. The second week I was there the therapist had me put my finger as close to my lips as I would dare and just hold it there for ten minutes. That was hard for me, but I did it.

The next session one of the women in the group put one of those Tic Tac candies on the floor. She said, "Gustina, eat that." Well now, that put me in a little bit of a bind because I didn't want to eat it, yet I knew it was OK to eat it. I remember that day distinctly. It was November 26, the Tuesday before Thanksgiving. I hemmed and hawed and I tried to back off a bit. Finally, without thinking I just grabbed it and put it into my mouth.

After that experience with the Tic Tac I began to work directly on my fear of eating apple pie and ice cream, and all the other major areas. I used to love apple pie and ice cream. That's as American as you can get. As I look back twenty-odd years, I think I felt I wasn't good enough to eat this dessert, I didn't deserve it. It had something to do with my lack of self-esteem. At the time I feared I might get anxious or depressed if I ate it. One night I stopped at a restaurant, ordered apple pie and ice cream, and ate the whole thing. It was actually the same night I ate that Tic Tac during the third group meeting. I left the meeting, went directly to a restaurant, and ordered apple pie and ice cream. I was taking one of the other members home. We stopped at a pancake house. I didn't even want to eat it because I was on a diet, but I figured I had to. Once I made my decision I wasn't even anxious.

The biggest turning point was putting that Tic Tac in my mouth after it had been on the floor. The next morning was the day before Thanksgiving. When I woke up I just felt I had done what I had done and no way was I going back. I didn't care what happened, there was no way I was going to turn back. I was unemployed at the time, but somehow or other I was feeling very positive about my future.

Later that day I decided to clean the rooms upstairs. Now you know I would never clean the house without great preparation. But on this day I felt strong and decided I would begin that task. Physically, I was about as tight as a rubber band. My leg muscles were aching. Of course I was confronting a very basic problem, but the thought of turning back did not even occur to me. I could have said, "You're getting a little too upset now. Maybe you should stop and just forget about it and try it another time." I counted on my ability to dissociate the OCD from any kind of emotion consciously. Certainly unconsciously I was as tight as hell. Consciously I talked to myself about how I could do it. In my mind I figured the group session the night before was just as if I had gone through surgery. I said, "I went through surgery yesterday, and today I am in the recovery room. Suppose I had had my gallbladder out. You suffer for a couple of days with that too, so this is just a typical reaction. I am in the recovery room, and I am going to get through this problem." I was bound and determined to push through, and so I did.

After cleaning for an hour or two I had to get ready for Thanksgiving dinner at my brother's. I remember that once arriving at his house I started pacing the floor. I thought to myself, "I'm having delirium tremors here. I'm having withdrawal." I told my brother, "I'm in the middle of giving up a lot of my rituals so you will have to tolerate me because I'm stressed out here and I need to walk this off." He said, "Gustina, remember that you are one day into your recovery. You're one day better." After being at my brother's for a while and talking openly with people who care about me, my anxiety began to go away. That was probably the worst day I had because I decided to give up one of the big ones, my cleaning rituals.

Touching food was the hardest ritual to face but also the most important one. I have always believed the dinner table is very important for family ties, but my children and I did not eat at the dinner table for eight years. I didn't mind so much when they lived at home, because I still got to see them. Once they moved out I felt highly motivated to gain control of my eating rituals so that I could enjoy meals with my children and grandchildren. In the back of my mind the dinner table is the tie that binds the family. I felt I needed to be able to invite my children and their families to dinner because I was living alone and wanted to maintain my family ties.

As it happens, I just accomplished this goal. I made vegetable soup a couple of weekends ago for the first time without washing my hands and without shopping for the food on a particular day. I prepared all the food. And I don't make just a little vegetable soup, I make a lot!

It was funny, though. I went through all this trouble to make my first meal without ritualizing. Then I called my daughter up to invite her and her husband for supper and she said, "Sorry, we can't come." But they did make it the next night. She was surprised when I sat down with them. "Oh, are you going to eat, too?" she asked. I said, "Well, yeah. You don't think I made this just for you, do you?" It was only a bowl of soup, but we ate it together and I was relaxed and without rituals. That was a big step for me.

I have a few suggestions for people who are just beginning to face their problems. As I said earlier, you need to deemotionalize your ritual. Don't look at it with any kind of emotion, just as an obsessive-compulsive ritual. The more you disassociate energy and emotion from it, the easier it is to handle. When your ritual is no longer associated with emotions, then you become logical. You are able to say, for instance, "This is just food." Now even when I see something that doesn't look quite right, I'll eat it.

You can't forget to practice your skills. Even though I declare that I am no longer going to do a certain ritual, that doesn't mean it's over and done with. I still work on it, and I probably will for the longest time be working on it. I've gotten to the point where I've forgotten half of the things I used to do, and hopefully I'll forget all of them. But until that point you do have to work on your rituals, because your behavior pattern has just been there for so long.

Some days there is a setback when rituals recur. This does not mean you are back at square one. It's just that when you are tired or lonely or in a stressful situation, the urge to do rituals becomes strong. It is important to remember it is not permanent and tomorrow is another day. Do not project your problems beyond today.

I think another key point is to find people who will support you through this whole project. For me it was the self-help group that was very important. I gained from listening to other people in the group, since many of them had learned through behavioral therapy. They were all average, normal, intelligent, fine, decent people who happened to have a problem. In some people it's a horrendous problem. As bad as mine was I was still able to function. I could still work. Even though I manipulated and maneuvered, I still managed to be able to feed myself. The group gave me a lot of support and let me know I was not the only one with the problem. I understood it is an illness and not some kind of wrongdoing on my part or any kind of moral thing. It has nothing to do with morality. It's an illness.

I guess I'm proof that it can be done away with, but you really have to want to work on it. You cannot make half-hearted efforts. You have to be really intent on your task. You can't just play around. If you are in a group, you can't just say, "Well, maybe I'll go this week and maybe I won't go." You have to dedicate yourself to getting better. You really have to want to get better. You may stop one ritual and in a month or two it will pop right back, so you have to be motivated, or little setbacks will discourage you.

Just be prepared for working hard and really meaning it. If you're messing around, you're messing around with the rest of your life. I figure I've got maybe twenty more years on this earth, give or take a few. No way do I want to live like that the rest of my life. I lived with OCD for almost half of my life already.

The group therapist once said that my grandson need never know that I've had OCD, and that just struck me. He's right. My grandkids are still just toddlers, and now OCD is over and done with for me. So they'll get to see a grandmother who acts normal and doesn't get stuck in the kitchen or have trouble leaving the bathroom.

Courage is relative. If you are not afraid of anything, then you can't be courageous. You are only courageous in relation to something you fear. If you fear getting out of bed in the morning and you get out of bed every morning, that's courage to me. I've been through it, so I know that sometimes getting up in the morning can take a hell of a lot of guts. It's much easier to just lie there forever and ever, amen.

A Last Word of Encouragement

As you can see, Shirley, Joel, Annette, Kate, and Gustina all suffered from severe OC problems. For years their obsessions and compulsions filled their waking hours with anguish and suffering. Before they joined the cognitive-behavioral program they were sure that they were doomed to a long life of misery. Yet they all found ways to challenge their so-called fate by taking a course of action that, in the short run, made them even *more* anxious and uncomfortable.

There are thousands of OC sufferers who have similar success stories. What do they all have in common? Shirley's following statement best captured the essence of her success: . . . *I just made up my mind that I was going to stop that kind of behavior. I decided I wasn't going to let something like that bother me, and that was all there was to it.* It was this attitude that enabled Shirley to follow the program diligently. She realized how strong her urge to ritualize was and she knew that she couldn't get better if her commitment for change was only tentative. Winning the battle required that she be persistent in following the *new* plan of action she adopted.

Again and again people with OCD prove that they can improve their lives dramatically by actively following through on their decision to give up their obsessions and compulsions. You too can join them by searching inside for strength and determination.

There is no need for you to tackle your problem alone. If you are hesitant to begin the program, or if you start losing your momentum after a few weeks, then seek the help of a trained mental-health professional, find out if there is a local support group for OCD, or ask a close friend to help you implement the self-help program. On the next page we have listed some resources that you might want to contact for more information.

RESOURCES

National Service Organizations

Two national organizations offer support for obsessive-compulsive disorder, including self-help booklets, information on forming self-help groups, and referrals to mental-health professionals. Both publish newsletters containing information about new research, treatment advances, and self-help techniques and programs.

The OCD Foundation
P.O. Box 9573
New Haven, CT 06535

The Anxiety Disorders Association of America
6000 Executive Blvd., Suite 200
Rockville, MD 20852-3081
301-231-9350

Clinics and Hospitals

For a current listing of hospitals, clinics, and university centers that specialize in OCD treatment and research, contact:

Center for the Treatment and Study of Anxiety
c/o EPPI Medical College of Pennsylvania
3200 Henry Avenue
Philadelphia, PA 19129
215-842-4010

Self-Help Tapes

For information on audiotapes that teach anxiety-reduction techniques, contact:

Health Psychology Tapes
P.O. Box 269
Chapel Hill, NC 27514
919-942-0700

Index

Page numbers of diagrams or tables appear in boldface

About the Authors

Edna B. Foa, Ph.D., is a professor in psychiatry at the Medical College of Pennsylvania and director of the Center for the Treatment and Study of Anxiety. She is an internationally renowned authority on the psychopathology and treatment of anxiety and one of the leading scientists in the area of obsessive-compulsive disorders (OCD). Dr. Foa has published over one hundred articles and several books on the topic. In addition, she lectures extensively around the world and is the chairperson of the DSM-IV committee on OCD.

Reid Wilson, Ph.D., is a clinical psychologist in private practice in Chapel Hill, North Carolina. Dr. Wilson is a member of the Board of Directors of the Anxiety Disorders Association of America and served for three years as the program chair of the National Conference on Anxiety Disorders. He is the author of *DON'T PANIC: Taking Control of Anxiety Attacks* and is a consultant for the airline industry in the treatment of fearful fliers.